"A scholarly work, cleverly written, full of the wisdom of the Power on High. This book is a truly effective transformative tool to bring us to our highest good."

– Vernon M. Sylvest, M.D.,
author of *The Formula;*
Medical Director, Lab Corp of America

"This book is a treasure of ancient mystery teachings for the committed student of higher consciousness. From wherever you are, it takes you to a new understanding of awareness and love."

– Rodney Charles,
Best-selling author of *Every Day a Miracle Happens*

"The power and depth of the technology and understanding presented in this book has made itself apparent in sessions with a very special group of patients. I have also applied it to my own life with great benefit. It works!"

– Raul Rodriquez, M.D.,
Medical Director, La Hacienda Treatment Center

"This book is a beacon of light that will reveal to you the eternal principles behind twelve universal truths and how to practically apply them to manifest your innermost values. Provocative and highly useful, it is full of uncommon insight. Here you have the sense that you have finally arrived. A great gift to humanity. This book is a must read!"

– Blanca Diez, M.D.,
Medical Director, New Horizons Treatment Center

✢ ✢ ✢

12 SECRETS *for* MANIFESTING *your* VISION, INSPIRATION & PURPOSE

HOW TO MAKE YOUR DREAMS COME TRUE

DR. D. RICHARD BELLAMY

PHI Publishing ✦ Houston, Texas

TWELVE SECRETS FOR MANIFESTING YOUR VISION, INSPIRATION & PURPOSE: HOW TO MAKE YOUR DREAMS COME TRUE © 1999 by Dr. D. Richard Bellamy

PHI Publishing
2400 Augusta Drive, Suite 210
Houston, TX 77057

Book design & copy editing by Sara Patton
Back cover copy by Susan Kendrick
Printed in the United States ✦ First printing 1999

ISBN 0-9662306-1-2
LIBRARY OF CONGRESS CATALOG CARD 98-065148

CONTENTS

Aka Nefer

Dedicated to the memories of my
beloved mother, Mary Ellen Bellamy,
and my dear friend, Andrea Blanche Hand.
Your lives touched many and you taught me
much about love . . .

To the great visionaries of philosophy
and science, whose shoulders I stand on . . .

And to all people of all nations, all races,
and all religions, today and tomorrow.

FOREWORD

This book is magnificent. There is that feeling of recognition — the special part of my mind that says, "Oh yes, that is right. That is true. And I already knew it."

This remarkable book is a treasure. The light of wisdom and intelligence shines here on the words of my lifelong friends of the mind: Ralph Waldo Emerson, Lao Tsu, Socrates, and many more are presented in this book in a wonderful way.

Dr. Richard Bellamy has discovered the universal principles which these great minds have given to us all. There is a pattern and a rhythm to these thoughts. One of my favorite authors, George Bernard Shaw, said, "I cannot teach you anything. I can only awaken you to what you already know." Dr. Bellamy reminds us that Socrates explained the same thought with, "All inquiry and all learning is but recollection."

I promise you this: your life, your heart, your mind will never be the same after you read this great book and work the exercises in it to manifest your own vision, inspiration, and purpose. You will treasure this book all of your life, because through it you will know that you belong in the company of the great thinkers. And best of all, you will realize that you already knew it.

– Dottie Walters, Publisher/Editor, *Sharing Ideas* magazine

MANIFESTATION FORMULA

Purpose

+

Thought

+

Vision

+

Affirmation

+

Feeling

+

Writing in Time and Space

+

Action with Energy on Matter

+

Gratitude

+

Perseverance

=

Manifestation

"Man is the rope stretched between the animal and the Superhuman."

– Friedrich Nietzsche

INTRODUCTION

The manifestation formula is a primary principle that exists today. It existed 5,000 years ago and it will still exist 5,000 years from now. You are a part of this time-tested equation. The formula only works, however, if you work the formula.

Although the manifestation formula has stood the test of time, I do not know who first conceptualized it, where they came from, or where they are now. I do know that it was taught by nutritionist and health proponent Paul Bragg, who was mentor to Dr. Jack LaLanne (the famous fitness proponent), and to my friend and mentor, Dr. John F. Demartini. Dr. Demartini further developed the formula and taught it to me. I, in turn, have added to and defined the formula for you.

My intention is to stretch your mind and open your heart by weaving a densely knitted fabric of great ideas that you can grab hold of. Ideas that you can use as a process to find your meaningful purpose in life, to clarify your thoughts, and to create and focus on your vision. My goal is to guide you so that you may hear your calling, and affirm it with words that are transformed in power by the feeling of love for who you are, where you came from, where you are heading, and what you are to do; and do so with such strong intent that you decide to give life to your idea by writing it down in tangible form, so you are compelled to take intense action, with energy on the matter at hand, with gratitude and perseverance until, during, and after you experience your purposeful manifestation.

In Plato's *Republic*, Socrates tells the story of a group of people who have spent their entire lives in an underground cave. They are bound by their necks and legs, facing the wall of the cave. A fire burns behind them, casting shadows on the walls. Their only concept of reality is their shadows on the wall. Socrates predicts that if one of them somehow became unbound and found himself ascending a steep, rugged passage to the outside, as he approached the light his eyes would be dazzled and he would not be able to see this new reality. He would require time to become accustomed to the world outside. First he would notice shadows, then reflections in the water, then objects themselves, then the light of the moon. Last of all, he would be able to see the sun. If he were to come back and tell the other cave dwellers of his discovery, the others, having known only the shadows on the wall, would probably not believe him. If he were to loosen their bindings and lead them out of the cave into the midday sun, the cave dwellers, being unaccustomed to the brightness, would probably squint, cover their eyes, and rush back into the cave, cursing the one who led them to the light. Great insights and ideas are first accommodated and then assimilated, and finally integrated.

As you begin to read this book, a part of you may feel that you have got to read it now. You may feel that you have to put it down for a while. You may say to yourself that you ought to go back, read this a second time, and go through the exercises again. You may feel that you should study this book intently. You may need to give it a rest. Perhaps you will feel drawn to read and complete the exercises with great attention to detail now.

Perhaps you will want to digest the information, or immediately begin to assimilate and use the information. You may choose to read this book rapidly and repeatedly until you get the big picture. You may choose to take it in slowly while reading between the lines with great understanding as you do the exercises. You may feel a desire to study this book at different times throughout your life.

You might find yourself choosing to go forward and upward in life as you read and apply this book again and again. You might discover that you choose to keep this book in some special place where you naturally let go of distractions and receive your intuition and inspiration. You might find that you love to read this book, or that you feel inspired as you do the exercises often in your quiet moments. You might become aware that you would love to share this book with others. *However you find yourself reading this book is perfect for you now.*

As you continue to read this book, I invite you to begin to remember how it feels when someone you admire and respect, inspires you. What position would you place your body in if you were reading an inspiring message from them? How would you breathe as you listen intently to the message? How surprised would you be to suddenly discover that the one you admire and respect the most is a still voice that speaks to you quietly as it flows from above to within your heart? You can let this still, calm voice guide you with intuitive wisdom and inspiration as you understand and take action on the ideas in each chapter of this book. Notice how your mind is open with total anticipation to receive the learning as you begin to allow the understanding to rise up from deep inside you now.

There are some people who say that how, what, and who you are, do, and have are determined totally by you. There are others who say that who you are, what you do, and what you have is totally determined by a power greater than yourself. Both are polarized beliefs. Who you are, what you do, and what you have is decided by your free-willed actions that are taken within the universal principles of nature's Divine design. Divine design is determined by an Omnipotent and Omniscient Presence that rules and guides us from a sphere of greater consciousness, above the paradox we call living. Make your freely willed actions a grand plan united with the Divine design.

‡ ‡ ‡

Throughout this book, the Omnipotent and Omniscient Presence will be referred to as the "Power on High." The free-willed part within each of us that chooses to move our striated, voluntary muscular system and directs our conscious actions will be referred to as the "power within." The primitive part of us that unconsciously regulates thought, respiration, digestion, endocrine, and unconscious nervous systems will be referred to as the "power below." Nietzsche wrote in *Thus Spoke Zarathustra*: "Man is a rope [power within] stretched between the animal [power below] and the Superhuman [Power on High]."

Why have I bothered to define the Power on High, the power within, and the power below? Because I have noticed that different writers use the same words to mean many different things. For example, if we look at the word "ego" as Sigmund Freud intended it, we can clearly see that he was describing the higher state of mind that I call the free-willed power within. If you read some of the popular writing of the present time you will see a different meaning of the word "ego" that I would describe as the power below.

Similarly, words such as "soul" (Plato describes three different types of souls), "spirit," and "subconscious" have different meanings implied by so many sources that I prefer to describe them within this book as the Power on High (the Omnipotent and Omniscient Presence that guides us from a sphere of greater consciousness), the power within (which consciously utilizes the more highly evolved and anatomically placed higher parts of our brain), and the power below (which is less evolved, controlling more primitive functions of our neuroendocrine system, and located lower and deeper anatomically in the nervous system). These descriptive names provide a simple nomenclature which I hope will enable you to more clearly understand what I mean.

Other words that you will encounter within these pages are as follows:

Bond angle: The angle of an attaching surface of a molecule, atom, or subatomic particle.

Frustum: A frustum is a horizontal plane at a specific vertical level on a cone or pyramid. Frustum, as used in this book, is a gradient level of being, doing, and having that we rise to, accommodate, and eventually rise above and beyond to the next level.

Myelinating: Derived from the word "myelin." Myelin is an insulating substance that wraps around the axon of neurons to enhance conduction of an action potential in a focused pathway. The more a sensory or motor axon is activated in a specific pathway, the more efficient it becomes at facilitating an action potential, because myelin guides the action potential along its pathway.

Phase lock: Two or more electromagnetic fields that resonate in phase, establish rapport with one another, come together, and lock as one.

Syntropy: In thermodynamics, entropy is described as going toward disorder, from *one* to *many*. Negentropy is described as going toward order, from *many* toward *one*. Entropy and negentropy are opposing forces that create a container of paradoxical relationship (paradigm).

Imagine syntropy as the bigger idea of a symmetrical relationship between entropy (disorder) and negentropy (order) that opens up to a new paradigmal sphere of influence that is greater in magnitude and relative order.

For example, imagine yourself suddenly transported to the moon. You find yourself standing on the lunar surface. As you look back through space, through the clouds around the earth, and see the bright blue oceans and dark land masses, you notice how the earth turns on its axis. You might find yourself realizing that the same earth you had previously thought of as being a dichotomy of chaos, has a higher, relatively more symmetric and orderly synthesis of entropy and negentropy (syntropy) that makes the earth appear so beautiful as you look down upon it. The term "syntropy" was originally coined by Buckminster Fuller.

Wavefront: The front surface of an electromagnetic wave that is the locus of all points having identical phase.

Enough of science class! I invite you to relax and enjoy the inner and outer journey as you read and do the exercises in each chapter. Imagine yourself in the future, having studied each chapter and completed the writing exercises, looking back on this moment and realizing that your life now has higher and higher levels of significance, meaning, and order. Now, returning to *this* moment, you find yourself experiencing infinitely more powerful levels of being, doing, and having, as you begin manifesting your vision, inspiration, and purpose now!

I recommend that you read each chapter at a leisurely pace before reading the next chapter, unless your intuition guides you to a specific page in the book. You may choose to write down any insights or inspirations you receive along the way.

Many are called but few are chosen
because the many are too distracted by pain
and pleasure to stand up and be chosen,
although the many are eternally called to be
delivered to the kingdom within the heart.

PURPOSE

Humans alone question their reason for existence. Our ability to ponder our existence differentiates us from animals. Once we answer the question of the meaning of our existence, we are united with the Divine.

Just as we (the power within us) use our primitive-minded innate inclinations, abilities, and talents to serve our own valued ends, our Power on High uses our free-willed, higher-minded power within to serve its purposeful ends. Pain and pleasure are the two balancing reins that the Power on High utilizes to steady the power within us and prevent us from going over the edge on the long spiraling road up the mountain of life.

If we set up pleasure as the meaning of our lives, we ensure that life will seem quite meaningless as we discover pain on the flip side of pleasure. Conversely, if we set up pain as the meaning of our lives, we ensure that life will seem quite meaningless as we discover pleasure on the flip side of pain. Pain and pleasure are necessary components that help manifest our coin of life. If we flip-flop our coin of life on the horizontal plane we discover extremes of pain or pleasure. We continue to flip-flop our coin of life until we become disillusioned, and then stop, and dissolve the illusive ions of our perceptions. If we raise our coin of

11

life on the vertical plane, we balance pain and pleasure and provide a connection for the Power on High to choose us.

Many are called but few are chosen, because many are too distracted by pain and pleasure to stand up on the vertical plane and be chosen, although the many are eternally called to be delivered to the Kingdom within the heart.

Unless we have an object of intangible value as our focus of attention, with intentional determination and deliberate resolution, we are like a ship of mutinous fools who have thrown the captain and navigator overboard. We are cursed to be pushed by the wind and pulled by the currents on a chaotic and uncertain journey.

In reality, most people will be pushed and pulled through life — some more than others—unconsciously reacting to the forces of their own making that create the tick-tock in their lives. They are not aware that they are born to be co-creators and that in fact they are. They do not see it because they are preoccupied with their role as victim-creature, and held there by lack of vision, inspiration, and purpose.

Our true destiny is to be co-creator with our Creator. We are a part of the greater whole, much like a wave is part of the ocean. As you visualize the last statement you can begin to understand that we are like a calm, placid, smooth-as-glass, rhythmic, symmetrical, proportionate surf when we are listening to our heart, the power within listening to the Power on High and following the straight and narrow path of our vision, inspiration, and purpose. We are "on the beam," listening to the inspiration of the Light and acting on it in understanding, certainty, gratitude, and inspiration.

To the degree that we are not in the flow with the great Source (the ocean of inspiration), we (the waves) experience turbulence, restlessness, and opposing forces of attraction and repulsion that, if strong enough, can propel us into a downward spiral of desperation. If we do not follow our inspiration, we wallow in desperation.

Nicholas of Cusa, a 13th-century philosopher and cardinal, said, "God creates the cosmos, we create the microcosmos." Physicists today state that in experiments with subatomic particles the outcome can be influenced by the thoughts of the experimenter. Genesis, Chapter 11, verse 6, states, "If people are of one mind and one language, nothing will prevent them from doing that which they have imagined to do." Buddha said, "When you fix your heart on one point, then nothing is impossible for you." Achievers have an attitude of expectancy because they have their hearts focused on their purpose, and their purpose is greater than themselves.

We cannot be focused on something greater than ourselves if we are preoccupied with the many fears of the future and guilts about the past. These fears and guilts drive us to lose our present-time consciousness by omitting what is purposeful (through inaction) or committing what is tangential to our purpose. Similarly, we cannot tune into the frequency of the station of the Power on High if we are distracted by the static of our fear and guilt-driven exaggerations and minimizations of what is, such that it keeps us from listening to our inspired, heartfelt messages.

When you are tuned into the frequency of the Light from on high, listening to your heart, following your bliss, filled with inspiration, and acting with faith, confidence, and certainty on what your gut instinct knows that your intuitive mind knows that your inspired heart knows is your purpose, the power of the universe supports you. You break the veil of the mundane world by magnetically attracting the people, places, ideas, and events to support you in your mission. You have created conscious spiritual force interacting with matter. You have synthesized opposing forces of nature without annihilating them. You have transcended the lower order to find yourself in the golden realm of purposeful being, doing, and having.

In Matthew 25:29 we read, "To every person who has something [purpose], more will be given, and he will have more than enough; but the person who has nothing [no purpose], even the little he has will be taken away from him." We have all been given a gift by our Master. Will we bury our talents because we fear losing them or do not feel worthy of them? Our purpose is a gift from our Power on High. To the degree that we are not following our purpose we are sabotaging our bodily form. To quote Dr. John Demartini, "Anything not on purpose will destroy itself in time and space." Lao Tsu said, "What is contrary to the Tao 'path' or 'way' soon comes to an end." If we pass the torch, we get more light. If we hide it under a basket, it burns out.

Every science I have studied has revealed that the universe is in motion. Every subatomic particle has interaction directed toward an ultimate purpose of becoming part of an atom; every cell has interaction directed toward a purpose of becoming a tissue; and so on. Every human being has interaction directed toward a purpose of becoming a spiritual being. If the cells of our body stop interacting toward becoming a tissue, they die. The degree to which we are not expressing life is the degree to which we are not interacting toward our purpose. We would be wiser to take the straight, vertical path of the Source instead of the horizontally, tangentially, spiraling, shadowy, stormy ride on the wild pendulum of emotional charge.

Many have said that nature (heredity) determines our destiny. Others have said that nurture (environment) determines our destiny. Both are partially right and partially wrong. Nature and nurture both give us our perceived voids, which birth our perceived values in life. If you link your creative values (goals) to your eternal value (purpose), and your situational values (action steps) to your eternal purposeful value and creative values, you have made a decision. Decision ultimately determines your destiny. Decide to follow your purpose today.

You may already be asking, "What is my purpose?" Clearly, I cannot answer your question. But *you* can, and I can help you in the process. Galileo said, "You cannot teach a man anything; you can only help him find it within himself." So I am much like a midwife and you—if you will indulge me—are pregnant with purpose. I will coax you to birth the realization of your purpose, provided you have felt the stirring within and are ready.

I invite you to look closely at the daily clues to your purpose. Every person, place, idea, situation, and experience that is a part of life and death has a meaning and serves a purpose. The more you acknowledge the meaning of these parts, the more meaning you add to the whole of your life.

Here is an example of this from personal experience. One morning, I was sitting with estate papers spread out across my mother's bed in Florence, South Carolina. My mother had moved into the house the week before, and then passed away a few days later. I had flown in from Houston immediately.

I was going through my mother's papers, and feeling sad that I would not see her smile, hear her voice, or feel her hugs ever again. Simultaneously, I could feel my mother's loving presence with me. I realized that even in her transition our loving bond was not broken.

As I was going through her checkbook, I discovered a check written for a large amount of money to a law firm. I called the law firm to inquire about the check, and was transferred to a woman named Teresa who explained that the check had been for the purchase of my mother's house. I was about to thank Teresa for her help and hang up when she mentioned that she had met a "Ricky" Bellamy about 25 years ago in Myrtle Beach. I told her that I had been called Ricky when I was a young boy. She asked whether I knew two brothers named Charles and Joe, and her brother Michael.

Then she began to relate events that had happened more than 25 years ago. "You probably don't remember me, and what you said probably wasn't significant to you, but it was significant to me. I was ten years old then. We were staying at a campground in Myrtle Beach. It must have been an older brother and kid sister kind of thing. I wanted to tag along and the boys shunned me. They said some unkind things, as adolescents sometimes do. I felt left out, hurt, and ugly. You saw that I was upset and came over to console me. I remember that you told me I would be beautiful when I grew up. I have remembered you and your words all my life. Through the years I have asked many people that I thought might know you, where you might be. I do not believe our conversation today was an accident."

Teresa went on to tell me about her brother Michael, her husband, and her two children. I was at a loss for words. She thanked me and we hung up. I went back to work on the estate papers and pondered what had just happened.

Within a few minutes I called Teresa back and told her she had made my day. She said that she would like to come by and see me on her lunch break. She came to my mother's house, gave me a hug, and we visited for a little while. I gave her a copy of a previous edition of this book and a tape of a radio interview I had given. I hope they will inspire her for at least another 25 years. Teresa confirmed my purpose, and for that I am grateful.

Can you begin to look back on your life and ponder what part of your life you felt had something missing? When did you perceive an apparent void because you felt a lack of something that you valued greatly? You might to this day find yourself remembering that void, having it pop into your mind frequently. It is not necessary to remember any void in your life now, but if you were to allow yourself to continue to wonder about it, could you imagine yourself mysteriously and suddenly realizing your deepest value now?

+ What has been the most important value perceived as missing in your life?

+ How can you use that void as fuel to propel you on your way to what you value most?

+ Who are you actually?

+ Where did you come from?

+ Where are you going?

+ Why are you here now?

+ Do you recall having an inspired calling, knowing, vision, or other peak experience as a child?

+ If so, what was it like?

+ What gives you and your life the most significance and meaning?

+ When are you most fulfilled?

+ What lights you up the most?

+ What inspires you?

+ Imagine if your life were a person, what would your life ask of you?

Suppose you were living your life over and could skip the distractive tangents, acting on purpose as you take action toward what you love now . . .

+ How would you be living?

+ Who would you be?

+ What would you be doing?

+ What would you have?

You might want to ponder these questions as you read this book. Feel free to return to them as often as it takes to get your answers. The more certainty you have of your answers, the more clear your purpose and the more power you generate toward fulfilling it.

✸ ✸ ✸

As you contemplate your purpose, realize that a purpose and a goal are not the same. Purpose is the *why* of life and goals are the *how*. When the purpose (why) is clear and true, the goals (how's) take care of themselves. Purpose is the ultimate, and it is relatively intangible; while goals are relatively tangible and transient.

Tangential creative values and transient situational values give us the passing ions of "passion," which give us the transient elations we may confuse with fulfillment. Purpose gives us fulfillment that has lasting significance and value that stands the test of time. To say it another way, a goal may be a fad or trend, and purpose is a classic. Anything you can achieve in your life is not really your purpose (although we may call it that); it is a higher-ordered goal linked to your ultimate valued purpose. Your ultimate valued purpose is transcendent to anything you accomplish.

Writing this book is part of my purpose to inspire, heal, write books and music, and teach in a way that has lasting significance and value that stands the test of time. The *purpose* of this book is that it will be read a thousand years from now and people will experience significance and meaning and receive benefit from it. My *goal* is that it will be quite successful now and sell a million copies overnight! My *why* for writing this book is that I received an inspiration and vision of it in a time of reflection and it is congruent with my purpose. The *how* is coming together based on the *why*.

In Plato's *Symposium*, the priestess Diotima, master of Socrates, instructs Socrates in understanding love and beauty. She explains that the essence is of a higher order than the form. Socrates himself explains in *The Republic* that if a globe's form (how) is destroyed, the mathematical principles (why) that describe the globe will endure. The principles of our purpose (our why) breathe life into our creations (our how). When the why is large enough, our how begins to take form.

Values with a meaningful purpose that focus on succession are more substantial in that they are lasting through time and space, approaching eternity and infinity, respectively. They are lasting in the space of our world by the greater hierarchical social levels they transcend. A purpose that affects its intention for a day can be said to be one level. A purpose that affects its intention for a year is yet another level. A purpose that affects its intention for a decade, a generation, a lifetime, or a century are all increasingly higher levels. A purpose that affects its intention for all time eternal is of the highest order. You can clearly see that a purpose that transcends time has more significance and meaning than one that is transcended by time.

Meaningful values with purposes that affect one person can be said to be one level. A purpose that affects its intention through a family is another level. Purposes that affect a city, a state or region, a country or continent, a hemisphere, the world, or the solar system are all increasingly higher levels. A purpose that affects the universe and beyond is of the highest order. You can clearly see that a purpose that transcends space has more significance and meaning than one that is transcended by space.

Can you begin to imagine what our ultimate purpose is? In Mark 12:28-32 we read, "And one of the scribes came near and heard them debating, and he saw that he gave them a good answer. So he asked him, 'Which is the first commandment of all?' Jesus said to him, 'The first of all commandments is, Hear, O Is-ra-el the Lord our God is one Lord; and you must love the Lord your God with all your soul and with all your mind and with all your might; this is the first commandment. And the second is like to it, 'You must love your neighbor as yourself. There is no other commandment greater than these.' The scribe said to him, 'Well Teacher, you have said the truth, that he is One, and there is no other besides him.' "

The word "Lord" has an archaic definition of "the head or master of a household," and the word "household" is defined as "a domestic establishment, including the members of a family and others living under the same roof." We can interpret the meaning of "Lord" as the head or master of a house or temple. The words "house" and "temple" can be interpreted in biblical writings as metaphors for the human form.

If we include this understanding in our reading of verses 29 through 31, we can begin to understand this passage as: "Hear O Is-ra-el the Master of your temple, the effect and manifested aspect of our God is One Master of our house [as opposed to many fragmented parts and pieces of our personality, called false personas and referred to in biblical writing as 'unclean spirits' or 'demons']. And you must love [accepting both sides of the coin of pleasure and pain, being thankful for what is, as it is] the Master of your temple, the force effect and manifested aspect of your God with all your soul [also called power within or higher mind] and your mind [also called the power below or lower mind] and with all your might [tremendous power experienced when the power within listens to its Master, the Power on High, and the power below listens to the power within and the three flow in symmetry, proportion, and order]. And the second is like to it, you must love [accepting both their perceived 'goods' and 'bads,' rising above out of judgment and separation and into unity and oneness] your neighbor [a reflection of yourself] as yourself [for to judge your neighbor is to judge yourself]."

When I lead Breakthrough Experiences and Vision, Inspiration, and Purpose (VIP) seminars, I ask the participants, "If you knew you had 24 hours to live, what would you do? How would you be? What would you have? What would you say? What would you say that you have not said? What are you afraid to say?" Suppose you were to ask these questions of yourself. What would your answers be? How surprised would you be to find yourself expressing love and gratitude to your friends, family, and Creator? Can you imagine what almost all participants in these seminars answer once they let their masks down and experience a moment of truth? If you imagine it is expressing unconditional love and gratitude for everyone, you are truly wise. Make an attitude of unconditional love and gratitude the solid rock foundation upon which you build your life.

Experiencing unconditional love and gratitude for what was, what is, and what will be our universe evolving around us, is the ultimate valued and meaningful purpose. Suppose you were to suddenly find yourself mysteriously becoming aware of the "big idea" whose time has come for you now. Imagine what would happen if you were to align and link your choices, desires, wants, needs, oughts, and haves to your spiritually inspired big idea that you would love to be, do, and have now. Make unconditional love and gratitude the hitching post of your choices, desires, wants, needs, oughts, and haves.

Imagine what it would feel like if your positively and negatively charged emotions—such as fear of the future and guilt about the past, false loves and false hates, expressed in your language as "always," "never," "all," and "none," and expressed in your body as underactivity and over-reactivity—were to come together at the center in pursuit of valued goals aligned with your purpose.

Your Power on High has gifted you with the breath of life for a purpose. In return, you can give no greater gift to your Power on High than to live your purpose. Every person has a unique purpose that has a single course up the middle golden line of purpose to the pole star above the mountain of life, and yours is no different. To the right is a line of pleasure, to the left a line of pain. Whether alone or together, the two are too weak to sustain you up the vertical path on the mountain of life. If the line of pleasure and the line of pain are brought to the center, and united with the line of purpose in a braided trinity, they will sustain you on the vertical path up the mountain.

Discover for yourself who you are and what has intrinsic value and meaning for you by embracing both pain and pleasure with focused thought on the vertical path of purpose. Do not ask for life to get easier; just ask for life to become more powerful in significance, meaning, and order. As you reach the top of your mountain, how surprised would you be to discover that the mountain was only a hill on a larger mountain? I encourage you to take aim on your pole star of purpose with focused thought like a laser point of light as you ascend the next mountain of life.

Whatever your innermost dominant thought is focused on is what you attract, move toward, or become.

Focus your thought like a laser point of light on your purposeful goals, objectives, and action steps.

THOUGHT

I had the opportunity to experience a nine-week transformational seminar when I was nineteen years old. This apparently cataclysmic and iconoclastic experience was compliments of the U.S. Navy. My first morning I was suddenly awakened at 4:30 a.m. by Petty Officer First Class Belton, who soon ordered us into the push-up position as he told us, "I'm going to teach you #!*&@% babies that *pain teaches dummies!*" I heard that statement many times over the next nine weeks, as we performed countless push-ups, sit-ups, and jumping jacks.

I resented Petty Officer Belton at the time. I did not like what I was feeling, but I had a purpose for being there. I had an intense desire to get a college education, compliments of the G.I. Bill. Whenever I was discouraged I focused my thoughts on my vision. I kept seeing myself in the future attending college. My silent mantra became G.I. Bill . . . G.I. Bill . . . G.I. Bill.

One time we were standing on the grinder at port arms with M-1 rifles, and Petty Officer Belton was reviewing us. I was on the front row. I don't remember what I did wrong, but he came up to me and yelled right in my face, "You #&*! head!" and adjusted my rifle position. He tapped me on the back of my right hand, which was holding the rifle butt, and drew blood.

I confess, my immediate thought (from the reptilian part of my mind) was that I could have easily hit him on the left side of his head with the butt of my rifle. But I did not. I wanted to achieve my objective. I started silently chanting G.I. Bill . . . G.I. Bill . . . G.I. Bill!

Have you ever noticed how time changes our perceptions? Today, I am truly grateful for this valuable lesson. This petty officer taught me to keep my thought on my purpose, my eye on my vision, and my inner voice on my mantra. Petty Officer Belton, if you ever read this, please know that I am truly grateful.

Have you ever considered that we are constantly manifesting our life as either creator or creature by demonstrating our thoughts in the form of the people, places, ideas, and events that appear in our lives? As we explore the formula for manifesting, we can easily realize that creators have clarity of vision, inspiration, and purpose; whereas creatures create with thoughts of relative lack of vision, desperation, and lack of purpose. Creators create with the synthesis of love, and creatures create with the polar extremes of fear and guilt, infatuation and resentment, exaggeration and minimization, omission and commission.

Deep layers of fears of the future and guilts about the past drive us to infatuation with or resentment of a person, place, idea, or event.

✦ Fear of the future drives us to become infatuated with a person, place, idea, or event we associate with pleasure.

✦ Guilt about the past drives us to resent and be repelled by a person, place, idea, or event we associate with pain.

✦ Fear of the future can also drive us to be repelled by (and move away from) a person, place, idea, or event that we associate with the loss of pleasure.

✦ And guilt about the past can drive us to become infatuated with (and move toward) a person, place, idea, or event we associate with the loss of pain.

Our exaggerations and minimizations are asymmetrically stored in our nervous system as polar electrical charges. They are manifested through our sensory and motor nervous system as excesses and deficiencies, and are based on our deep fears and guilts. These excesses and deficiencies manifest as omissions and commissions. When we are in omission we are in deficiency: neglecting or failing to do what is purposeful. When we are in commission we are in excess: reacting away from, and tangential or perpendicular to, what is purposeful.

Whenever we are infatuated with a person, place, idea, or event, we are possessed with an unreasoning passion and attraction to an object. To the degree we are infatuated, an equal and opposite degree of reaction (in the form of resentment) can be predicted to occur in time and space. The degree to which we are infatuated with a person, place, or thing is the degree to which we "lie" to ourselves.

Whenever we are resentful of a person, place, idea, or event, we feel indignantly aggrieved by an act, situation, or person, and are repulsed by the object. To the degree we are resentful, an equal and opposite degree of reaction (in the form of infatuation) can be predicted to occur in time and space. The degree to which we are resentful of a person, act, or situation is the degree to which we "lie" to ourselves.

Whenever we are infatuated with or resentful of a person, place, idea, or event, it is because we have either exaggerated something about an object or we have minimized something about it.

✦ We exaggerate about people, places, ideas, and events by magnifying things beyond proportion and beyond truth. In this case we distort through overstatement.

✦ We minimize people, places, ideas, and events by representing something as having the least degree of importance or value. In this case we distort through depreciation.

Infatuations are exaggerations of "goods" and minimizations of "bads" about people, places, events, ideas, and things. Resentments are minimizations of "goods" and exaggerations of "bads" about people, places, events, ideas, and things. Infatuations and resentments are "lies." You can begin to clearly understand that fears and guilts, infatuations and resentments, exaggerations and minimizations, elations and depressions, omissions and commissions give birth to further cycles of fears and guilts, infatuations and resentments, exaggerations and minimizations, elations and depressions, and omissions and commissions.

Remember the saying, "If you tell a lie then you will have to tell more lies to cover up the first lie"? As you begin to imagine layers upon layers of lies or false personas, I invite you to picture the higher-minded heart listening to the Power of the Light and Sound from on High as one in unity and purpose. As the higher-minded power within, of its free will, listens to the lower-minded power below, we find ourselves separated from our One True Being, birthing one entity of false being. This entity or "lie" is propped up by a two-member support group (false personas) of exaggeration and minimization in the form of bipolar extremes of infatuation and resentment fueled by fear and guilt.

+ This first lie births a generation of seven lies (or exaggerations and minimizations) to sustain and cover the first lie.

+ The seven lies birth a generation of 49 lies.

+ The 49 lies birth a generation of 343 lies.

+ The 343 lies birth a generation of 2,401 lies.

+ The 2,401 lies birth a generation of 16,807 lies.

+ The 16,807 lies birth a generation of 117,649 lies.

+ The 117,649 lies give birth to a legion of 823,543 scattered parts, pieces, and fragments.

The legion of lies blots out the Light from on High to the power within like the moon eclipses the sun. We find ourselves feeling as if the weight of the world is on our shoulders as we horizontally wallow, brokenhearted, in our self-pity, and react in our drama of perceived trauma. We find ourselves in desperation, cut off from our inspiration of the Power on High by the many false personas that fog our thinking. We find ourselves tuning to obstruction and interference by the asymmetrical electrical charges of static. We are unable to link up with the Power on High. The Light from on High is distorted by our legion of personas piled high and deep.

We find ourselves unconsciously unconscious as we react throughout life. Our deepest question seems to be, *How do I survive?* We seek pleasure and receive pain as we hit the wall of frustration we mistook for a door. The walls in our life have been laid down by the Power from on High as it projects its guiding Light, enveloping us in its cone of influence.

Imagine a pendulum hanging down from the apex of the Source of Light. As you begin to picture the pendulum swinging to and fro, you find yourself beginning to understand that the degree of the swings to and fro are directly proportional to the degree of emotional charges of the polarities of fear and guilt, infatuation and resentment, exaggeration and minimization, omission and commission, which are felt and expressed by each of us in our lives.

As the pendulum swings through the time and space we know as our lives, we can realize that when we swing to the edge of the cone of light and hit the wall of darkness we create an opposing wave. The pendulum shifts back to the opposite side and creates a wave. The waves opposing the pendulum (and each other) in its swing represent the turbulence we experience and express in our lives. The opposing waves of omission and commission eventually unite as one as they collapse inward to the middle, straight and narrow path. We (logarithmically approaching total perception of the Light on High) glimpse the light and peel off one quantum of false personas (for example, from 823,543 down to 117,649). The pendulum, having ascended vertically, swings to a slightly lesser degree. We feel lighter as we begin to stir from our horizontal frustum of existence to crawl from the depths of the deep to become semiconsciously unconscious.

We find ourselves semiconsciously unconscious: upset that we are disturbed, but without knowing what to do about it. We hear the "woulda's, shoulda's, coulda's" dancing in our head. Our deepest question seems to be, *What should I do?* We pass through the time and space of our lives reacting to our fears and guilts evolving as we experience both pain and pleasure. The Power on High is ever shining, waiting patiently beyond time and space as we follow our distractions. The power within listening to the power below distracts itself by seeking pleasure and avoiding pain, only to find that pain follows pleasure as surely as night follows day.

You can begin to understand that pain serves its purpose of counteracting the imbalance of our illusional, monopolar infatuation with pleasure. Everything in the universe is seeking balance toward unity. Why would the human mind be any different? I invite you to realize the obvious answer. You can clearly understand that the laws of thought follow the same laws of attraction and repulsion culminating in collapse of charge, as evidenced in subatomic physics all the way through astrophysics. You may not feel you ought to accept the idea that there are universal laws woven in the alpha through the omega through the alpha in endless continuum, but if you were to begin to think about it and consider the evidence, you might be surprised to find that you are indeed open to the possibility.

Pain serves as a correcting mechanism to bring us back toward our purpose by humbling us and leading us to begin to listen to our mission from the Power on High as we are at the level of semiconsciously unconscious. We compulsively seek pleasure to forget our pain, and we find ourselves molded by the events in our lives that cause us to change our minds as we peel off another quantum of personas. We leave the swamp to find ourselves on firmer ground as we evolve to semiconsciously semiconscious.

We find ourselves semiconsciously semiconscious, less disturbed by our disturbance. Our deepest question seems to be, *What do I need?* We have moments of clarity interspersed with moments of reptilian-like rage. We seek the security of our den, deeply covered, as we are reactive and not yet adaptive to our environment. We evolve through time and space, evolving beyond our reactions, transcending our environment as we crawl along, sometimes reacting, sometimes acting, on our way. And we peel off another quantum of personas and evolve to another frustum of consciously semiconscious.

We find ourselves consciously semiconscious. Our deepest question seems to be, *What do I want?* We evolve in cycles of spreading our wings and flying toward the tree of wisdom that is rooted in the Power on High, resting in its tributaries of branches and waddling along on the horizontal plane. We leave the security of our nest below the earth to seek a nest that rests in the branches above the earth. We feel the urge to attack those whom we judge to be less evolved than us—much like a bird dives for a snake—only to discover that we are attacking reflections of ourselves that we would rather not admit are reflections of ourselves. As we evolve through life, experiencing our pendulum swings between self-aggrandizement and self-depreciation, modulated by pain and pleasure, our opinions begin to collapse further as we shed another quantum and evolve to the frustum of consciously conscious.

We find ourselves consciously conscious, realizing that the way things *seem* to be seems all right, and yet we know we have a way to go in our evolution. Our deepest question seems to be, *What do I desire?* We migrate toward our perceived greener pasture of easy grazing. We are surprised to find a predator stalking us as its perceived tasty morsel. No matter who wins the predator and prey game, our winnings are transient. Then we find we have become the predator, and perpetrate on another what we have been through, until we begin to stop, look, listen, and understand as we are drawn to the tree of wisdom and we peel off another quantum of false personas. We evolve to superconsciously conscious.

We find ourselves superconsciously conscious. Our deepest question seems to be, *What do I choose?* We can choose to think of our existence in the universe as meaningless and irrational, or we can begin to notice that things have a purpose in being the way they are. We begin to look back on our past with understanding, love, and acceptance for what is, as it is. Having transcended many levels in our evolutionary spiral, we find ourselves masters of the levels we have transcended, not by brute force but by our intellect. We find our thinking clearer than at the levels we have transcended, and yet we continue to experience fears and guilts, infatuations and resentments, exaggerations and minimizations. We modulate them with action more than we exacerbate them with reaction. Our polar swings are much smaller now and evolve to the point that the chatter subsides and the power within becomes One with the Power on High. The still, quiet voice is heard, as soft and clear as a lamb. The lion-like roar is silenced as it bows to the power within and lies down at its feet. We cast off our final quantum of personas as we evolve to realize our One True Being.

Superconsciously superconscious, we accept things as they are, for we know we have participated in their creation. We know what we love with certainty. We are as focused as a laser point of light on what we love. We are free from distraction, even though each level of mass consciousness we have transcended both praises us to the point of worship with adoring reverence and regard, and reprimands us to the point of crucifixion with criticism, attempted persecution, and torment. We are neither infatuated nor resentful of either, as we see the perfection and are grateful for both. We accept both pain and pleasure as we focus and create with purpose, moving with poised elegance and attractive ease in our actions. It is clearly the hero's journey to fall from grace, from the One to the many, and be resurrected back to the One in grace, as we evolve back up the spiraling staircase from reacting to acting to being.

You can begin to understand that still water, not a restless stream, is used for a mirror. When the power within is clear and focused and the attention is even, it is then possible to discern true conditions. Like a glass of muddy water, the vital spirit, the power within, is hard to clarify and easy to muddle. Truth unfolds gradually, like a rose. Live in such a manner today that you welcome another degree of truth tomorrow.

When we finally decide to choose to listen to the Power on High, with temperate, subdued quietness, free from excess, extravagance, or exaggeration of opinions, showing sane and rational self-control, this is the point at which our heart opens and we are ushered with purpose up the mountain, to be inspired with a vision beyond the horizons of fear and guilt. We see the past and future simultaneously with present-time consciousness, as we birth a transformed memory and imagination, and begin to remember who we are and imagine what we are to do. We are filled with tears of gratitude as we give thanks to the Power on High.

"When thine eye is single
thy whole body also
is full of light."

– Luke 11:34

3
VISION

One morning, while staying in the Sinai region of Egypt, we arose at 2:00 am to begin our walk up Mount Sinai. If we hurried, we would reach the top in time for sunrise.

As we walked up the mountain, I began to peel off layers of clothes. It was a steep walk and I had begun to perspire, despite the 40-degree temperature. Along the way, some Bedouins offered the services of their camel for $20, calling out to us, "Good camel! Good camel!"

After quite some time, I reached the top of the mountain. I waited in a small Bedouin shack trying to warm up. As the edges of the horizon began to glow with the rose color of dawn, I looked into the east. There was a rather sudden rise of what looked to me like golden leaves blowing in the wind. Then I perceived a fiery bush. I was struck with awe by this event. After the sun had risen, I remembered that Moses had been so inspired by this vision that he united a nation and changed the course of history.

Purpose gives us a target of reference toward which we aim our thoughts. Symmetrical clarity of thought allows us to focus our attention alertly on our purpose, birthing our imaginative, anticipative conception of our vision of extraordinary beauty.

Vision is birthed by memory and imagination. Memory is distorted by guilt. Imagination is stifled by fear. Distorted memory and stifled imagination cause vision to perish. "Where there is no vision, the people perish." [Proverbs 29:18] Where there is vision, we flourish with abundance.

In Plato's book, *Meno,* we read the words of Socrates to Meno: "The soul, being immortal, and having been again many times, and having seen all things that exist . . . has knowledge of them all and it is no wonder that she should be able to call to remembrance all that she ever knew about virtue, and about everything; for as all nature is akin, and the soul has learned all things, there is no difficulty in her eliciting, or . . . learning, out of a single recollection all the rest, *if a man* [*or woman*] *is strenuous and does not faint,* for all inquiry and all learning is but recollection." Realize that you cannot see your future clearly until you see your past clearly, in detail, with symmetry, proportion, and order.

Plato's doctrine of reminiscence teaches that all learning is a kind of *remembering* of knowledge that is already present in the power within us. Socrates demonstrates to Meno that close examination in the search for truth, knowledge, comprehension, and mastery through experience or study are but the recalling to mind from the memory of the power within.

In reading Plato, it can be confusing to see the word "soul" used for different meanings. Some people have used the words "vegetative," "sensitive," and "rational" to describe three types of souls. The vegetative soul is analogous to the lower-minded power below. The sensitive soul is analogous to the higher-minded power within. And the rational soul is analogous to the Power on High.

If we include this understanding in our reading of the quotation from *Meno,* we can begin to understand it as follows:

38

"The soul [power within that is in time and space and is a pro-jection of the Power on High, which is beyond time and space], being immortal, and having been again many times, and hav-ing seen all things that exist . . . has knowledge of them all and it is no wonder that she [the power within] should be able to call to remembrance all that she ever knew about virtue, and about everything; for as all nature is akin and the soul has learned all things, there is no difficulty in her [the power within] eliciting, or . . . learning, out of a single recollection [from the Power on High] all the rest, if a man [or woman] can be stren-uous [vigorously strong in the free will of the power within] and does not faint [submit to the power below], for all inquiry and all learning is but recollection."

Future fears and past guilts are interdependently dynamic. One cannot exist without the other. Fear cannot exist without guilt and guilt cannot exist without fear. The lower-minded power below extrapolates from past experience, assuming that future events will conform to that pattern. To have guilt about the past is to expend energy that could be more purposefully directed. To have guilt about the past is to expend our precious, conscious attention non-locally through time, to manifest fear of the future proportionate to the degree of our perception of guilt.

We camouflage our guilts by projecting judgment onto others. When we are in judgment of self or others we are exag-gerating or minimizing what is, as it is, about a person, place, idea, or event. We manifest through the lower-minded power below an entity that exists as a distinct and self-contained unit of past guilts and future fears. The entity's top priority is self-preservation. The fragments of the false ego, called "false personas," project their judgments on people, places, ideas, or events in order to prevent annihilation by the Light of Truth.

These fragmented parts of our false ego sense their mortality as we awaken. These fragmented parts of us keep us from our vision that is aligned with our inspiration and purpose, by keeping our attention on the judgments we perceive. Our judgments summate to distract, distort, and shut us out from our vision aligned with inspiration and purpose much like leaves on a tree summate to distract, distort, and shut out the sun's light from our perception.

Our summated judgments keep our vision scattered on the many tangential rays that vie for our attention. What we focus on with infinite detail is what we attract. Notice that as we focus on what we cyclically infatuate and resent, exaggerate and minimize, we ionically attract and move toward what we cyclically infatuate and resent, exaggerate and minimize.

Clearly, what we see is what we get. Distractedly scattered with confusion and in the shadows, we stumble off course until we decide to stop, look up, and recognize what is before our eyes. We discover that what is hidden is revealed to us. The sacred vision appears as memory, and imagination achieves unusual depth to the point that it transcends time and space and projectively materializes on the movie screen of our minds.

We perceive through our lower-minded power below, via our senses, by noticing differences between stimuli. We compare and contrast. We note asymmetry, disproportions, disorder, and dis-ease. These perceptions serve a purpose by keeping our vehicle, the lower-minded power below, out of harm's way. This is as it is meant to be.

The higher-minded power within, through the Power on High, sees the unity of the apparent opposition. The power within perceives and resonates with the symmetry, the proportion, the order, and the precision that exists in all things. Consider that approximately 2,500 years ago Socrates said,

"Measure and symmetry are beauty and virtue the world over."
Plato wrote, "The beautiful never lacks proportion." Aristotle
wrote that beauty is "order, symmetry, and precision." Diotima
instructed Socrates, "At last the vision is revealed to him of a
single science, which is the science of beauty everywhere."

The lower-minded power below is the student of the
higher-minded power within. When the power within listens to
its master, the Power on High, and wisely instructs the power
below, there is order. When the power within listens to the
power below, which is guided by the senses, there is chaos.
When the higher-minded power within listens to the heartfelt
message of its master, the Power on High, and the lower-minded
power below listens to the higher-minded message of *its* master,
the power within, and the dualistic senses listen to *their* master,
the power below, a divinely guided unified force of vision is
birthed.

In Plotinus' *The Enneads* we read, "Shut your eyes and
change to and wake another way of seeing which everyone has,
but few use." The ancient Taoist sage, Lao Tzu, said, "Straighten
your body, unify your vision, and the harmony of heaven will
arrive." In Luke 11:34 we read, "When thine eye is single thy
whole body also is full of light." As you discover that memory
and imagination run the world, I invite you to begin to imagine,
to the point that you can easily visualize what you would love
to be, do, and have in infinite detail.

✠ ✠ ✠

Suppose you were to visualize your symmetrically pro-
portioned body that you are manifesting as you begin to take
action by breathing deeply, eating wisely, stretching gently and
slowly, working out intensely with weights, running moderately,

and taking long, invigorating walks. You find yourself feeling vibrant, magnetic, and the picture of health.

What would it feel like if you could imagine yourself writing a book? How surprised would you be to see the chapters completed and the book's title? Visualize a thousand years in the future, on a faraway planet such as Mars, and imagine what it would feel like to see a young man inside a building, sitting at a desk, inspired by a book he is reading. As your eyes focus on the title of the book, you realize the author is you.

Suppose you were to visualize to the point that you could see yourself creating a great work of music. As you find yourself hearing the music, you feel the electricity of inspiration surge through you as you mysteriously know that your music will stand the test of time and become a classic.

You might picture yourself with financial wealth, which you are easily attracting and building, as you conceive in vividly clear detail the many sources and action steps your wealth will easily and continuously flow from. Imagine how this will allow you to fulfill your purpose, leaving an immortal effect.

Begin to visualize your ideal companion and imagine what it would feel like to be with this person. You might find yourself picturing, clearly and easily, every detail to the point that you begin to notice shared values expressed in action by your ideal companion, creating a fantastically connected feeling. As you continue to picture their ideal eyes you notice their depth and color. As you continue to imagine, you see yourself discovering every detail of your ideal companion's facial features (lips, chin, nose, forehead) and hair color and texture.

What is it like when you begin to conceive to the point that you can clearly picture your ideal companion's body build? As you begin to perceive every line, curve, and angle, you can clearly discover the beauty of proportionate symmetry and balanced order. If you could hear your ideal companion's voice, what would it sound like and what would they say?

Now look back on all these details of your ideal companion and discover the total synergy. You can begin to experience an incredible connection with absolute fascination, to the point that you naturally realize you share the same values (such as respect, trust, communication, fun, and passion). Imagine what it would feel like as you readily picture the two of you and your relationship unfolding with significance, meaning, and love transcending time.

Suppose you were to imagine your ideal home. As you begin to picture this in detail, notice its location. As you begin to clearly see the perfect location of your ideal home, then imagine yourself noticing every detail—from the foundation and the superstructure to the floor covering, ceiling molding, and furniture—all expressing self-replicating symmetry that appeals to your internal sense of balance and harmony.

You might see yourself imagining your son or daughter as you expose them to the immortal classics of music, art, and literature. Continue to imagine them in the future, and clearly picture them following their heart, inspired with vision, inspiration, and purpose, and following the path they watched you climb. You see them looking back on this moment now as the beginning of an incredibly wonderful life.

Perhaps you have perceived yourself as less than outgoing in social situations. But suppose you were to stop and begin to see yourself in a different light, to the point that you discover a warm spotlight shining down on you from above. As the cone of luxurious light shines brightly, you begin to see yourself as a radiant being, magnetically attracting and moving toward the ideal people who align with your innermost dominant desires, choices, and loves.

Notice what it is like as you ever so finely tune into your spiritual nature, to the point that you can instantaneously look back on your life now, and find yourself reconsidering people, places, ideas, and events you once perceived as traumatic or bad. You can have the courageous state of mind that enables you to begin to think about them differently and see them in a whole new way, to the point that you naturally see the beautiful symmetry, proportion, and order, and you find yourself resurrected from the shadows and illuminated with vision by the Light from on High. You feel your heart open infinitely, and you immediately feel tears of bliss bursting forth and overflowing in abundance as you follow your higher-minded heart, inspired with gratitude, vision, and purpose.

You may not feel you need to drop your judgments immediately. But if you *did* begin to let them go, how surprised would you be to experience crystal-clear vision now? Imagine what would happen if you were to suddenly have the courage to stop and experience absolute clarity as you envision with detail, to the point that you take action with energy now.

William Blake said, "The world of imagination is the world of eternity. It is the divine bosom into which we shall all go after the death of the vegetative body." It has been said, "God is in the details." Can you imagine the infinitely detailed imagination and love our Creator focuses on—from the subatomic particles, to the atoms, molecules, cells, tissues, organs, and systems—to create you? Have you ever considered the infinite detail, imagination, and love the Creator focuses on to create the earth, the moon, the planets, the sun, the 200-billion-plus stars of the Milky Way galaxy, all galaxies, the universe, all universes?

In Psalms 115:16 we read, "Heaven belongs to the Lord alone, but he gave the earth to man." As you ponder that, you can begin to realize that it is our destiny to co-create with love and detail. Infinite love and infinite detail help you to hold your image.

I invite you to continue to grow in strength and intensity of illumination to the point that your whole being is instantaneously transformed from above, down, inside, and out. Your being is so bright that you see the infinitely precise, symmetrical, proportionate, and orderly beauty. The horizontally ordinary around you mysteriously births the process of uniting past memory and future imagination to the point of becoming one in present-time consciousness now, while you are illuminated to such a degree that the sacred, extraordinary, unified, and beautiful vision appears vertically in infinite brilliance, clarity, and detail. You are moved to such tremendous love and gratitude that you find yourself immediately affirming the message of your words of power with love as you readily write them down and take action with energy now.

What you talk about reinforces what you think about; therefore, it influences what you bring about. Affirm your meaningful purpose, not your future fears and past guilts.

AFFIRMATION

Have you ever considered that we are attracting or heading toward becoming, doing, or having the deepest, most inner, dominant thought of our power within? As you ponder the last statement, I invite you to begin to understand that within every thought is a recapitulation of all your thoughts up to this moment in time. Each thought we have today is dependent on the thoughts we had yesterday and backward in time infinitely. Each thought we have today will determine our thoughts tomorrow and forward in time infinitely. Every moment comes and goes, lives and dies, to be reborn in the next moment. You can easily realize that the present moment is a most important moment in determining your destiny.

When we think about the future, it is not the future, but the present moment in time inventing a possible future. When we think about the past, it is not the past, but the present moment in time recalling the past as we perceive it. The only moment we will ever have is this moment now. Our "now" becomes larger, brighter, and more detailed in proportion to the degree that we recall the past as it was and is, not as we illusionally perceive it. Our now becomes larger, brighter, and more detailed in proportion to the degree that we imagine the future unfolding and delivering our vision which is aligned with our purpose. Our now becomes smaller, darker, and fuzzier in proportion to the degree that we feel unworthy, as we recall the past with guilt due to our misperception of asymmetry, disproportion, and disorder. Our now becomes smaller, darker, and fuzzier in proportion to the degree that we stifle with future fear our vision that is aligned with our purpose.

We are on our way to becoming, doing, and having what we hear, see, and feel ourselves being, doing, and having. The outer conditions of a person's life will be in harmony with the inner state of both the higher-minded power within and the lower-minded power below. A tiny seed of thought birthed by the galactically inspired power within and planted in the earthly power below, when it is watered with attention and fertilized with action by the will of the power within directing the vehicular power below, does blossom into full flower. When we learn to use our power within properly, we will find that the choices and decisions made by our power within are guided and influenced by the knowing received from our Power on High.

The Power on High, being beyond time and space, being by our perception infinitely patient and without opinion, sees the symmetry, proportion, and order in our lives. It serves to empower us with its authority if we will tune to its frequency. To carry out with success and bring to pass our accomplishment we must stay on the path of purpose, while focusing our attention on our crystal-clear vision, with the patience of the Power on High through our power within, until our desire takes form. After our desire takes form, we must maintain our thought in order to maintain the form.

The power below tends to react to what it does not understand, and act on what it does understand. Repetition leads to familiarity. Familiarity ultimately leads to understanding.

Repetition serves to make an idea clearer to the power within and the power below. (In fact, for this reason I recommend that you read this book at least a dozen times.) Repetition wears down the resistance of electrical charge (static) that is conflicting or contrary to our affirmation. Repetition carries us past the initial, mutinous, reactive outburst of the power below and on to reinforce the inspiration of the higher-minded power within. The initial, mutinous outburst of the power below is quieted through time as the power within becomes stronger in its conviction. Spaced repetition through time leads us to learn, act, and become in time. Manifestation can only occur once we convince ourselves. I invite you to understand that a conviction will truly arise in us if we will speak our affirmations daily, hear our affirmations daily, read our affirmations daily, write our affirmations daily, and act on our affirmations daily.

How surprised would you be to understand that every statement we make to ourselves and others leaves an imprint in the form of a physical alteration occurring in neural tissue? If a true or false statement is repeated over time, we begin to believe it and find ourselves in a "rut." This is how we begin to believe our exaggerations and minimizations, our lies. If we wish to manifest what we would love, we must be accurate and truthful with all our statements. Words such as "always" or "never" are often exaggerations and minimizations of what is, and denote an emotional charge toward less purposeful tangents. "Always" is rarely true and "never" is usually false.

Suppose you were to tape record your conversations for three days. If you were to listen to the tapes, how surprised would you be to discover the exaggerations and minimizations in your language? How surprised would you be to hear the charged self-talk in your statements? Imagine what might happen if you were to write a list of the exaggerations and minimizations and charged self-talk that you use in your conversations, and take concerted action with energy to change it. If the power within—through the striated, voluntary muscles of the vocal cords—plants fear and guilt in the form of anger, resentment, envy, infatuation, exaggeration, minimization, omission, and commission in itself and the power below (remember, the power within is the teacher to the power below), we will harvest what we have planted. You can easily realize that we perform, become, and obtain what we think and talk about.

In the 15th chapter of Matthew, verse 11, we read, "Not what goes into the mouth defiles a man, but what comes out of the mouth, that is what defiles a man." In the 12th chapter of Matthew, verses 36–37, we read, "Every idle word men may speak they will give account in the day of judgment. For by your words you will be justified and by your words you will be condemned."

You can begin to realize that the non-purposeful words we speak debase, corrupt, and desecrate our higher-minded attention from our divinely inspired purpose. We will answer for our lazy chatter in the day of discerning self-judgment. No one will judge you more than you judge yourself.

You can clearly understand that the day of self-judgment begins and continues now, both forward and backward in our perception of time. You can continue to understand that we are doomed to a seeming eternity of self-judgment if we miss the mark and move in the horizontal plane. I invite you to discover that we are justifiably saved from the guilt and the penalty in the abode of the dead-ended horizontal plane and resurrected on the vertical plane as we affirm our words of power.

The Book of Job, chapter 22, verse 28, states, "Thou shalt decree a thing and it shall be established unto thee and the light shall shine upon your ways."

The Gospel of Thomas, verse 48, states, "If two [power within and power below] make peace with each other in this one house [body], they will say to the mountain, '[problem] move away', and it will move away."

The Gospel of Thomas, verse 106, states, "When you make the two one [spirit and matter, or power within and power below, become one], you will become the sons of man, and when you say, 'Mountain move away,' it will move away."

I invite you to understand that spirit without matter appears motionless to our senses, and matter without spirit is lifeless to our senses. Eventually, you can become truly aware that the Power on High does not have an opinion (opine-ion) about your life. It simply loves from a larger sphere of influence than you. It is tuned to you, to empower you to be, do, and have what you need, want, desire, choose, and love. To be, do, and have what you love, you must focus on what you love to be, do, and have to such a degree that you become so devoted to the cause that eventually the effect materializes.

I invite you to realize that we govern our words with our thoughts, and we govern our lives with our words. How surprised would you be to discover that we reinforce our thoughts with our words? Can you imagine what would happen if you were to govern your words with love for your purpose? Imagine the power you would feel in your words of power to the point that your word becomes a lawfully declared rule, established by the authority on high, which is not to be questioned or disputed. I encourage you to begin to speak your words of power today. As you continue your evolution of your affirmations, you can imagine the process as similar to sharpening a pencil. As you speak, write, and record your affirmations, you begin to discover incredible clarity of vision, truly focused thought, and unlimited purpose unfolding to such a degree that you find your words take on a new meaning, value, and depth to such a point of sharpness that your words suddenly become sacred words of power that inspire you to love and gratitude, united with action, immediately.

Have you ever spoken to yourself in the mirror? Suppose you were to say your words of power as you look at yourself in the mirror. Imagine what it would feel like if you were to speak your words of power as you stare at yourself in your left eye. Suppose you were to proclaim your words of power as you stare at yourself in the right eye. Suppose you were to declare your words of power as you intensely focus on the spot between your eyes above the bridge of your nose.

I encourage you to also write your affirmations with both your dominant and non-dominant hand at least seven times each.

Suppose you were to find yourself listening to a recording of your voice saying your affirmations. Imagine what it would feel like if you were to hear a recording of the voice of someone you respect saying your affirmations.

As you begin to speak, write, and listen to your affirmations, imagine that all at once you are seeing your favorite view; hearing your favorite, most inspiring music; breathing diaphragmatically and deeply; smelling your favorite smell; tasting your favorite, most exquisite taste; touching your fingers together as if you are rolling prayer beads through your fingers; and feeling your most inspiring feeling of gratitude. Your head is held high, your being is centered, and your eyes are closed (provided you are not reading or writing). You can easily see that the synaptic pathways that fire together will eventually wire together and summate their effect.

Realize that the more wordy your affirmations, the more scattered your thoughts. Say what you say as concisely and as meaningfully as you can, expressing much in a few succinct words. Intensity of words for immensity of conviction with brevity equals words of power. Realize that the more succinct your words, the more focused and profound your thought.

Begin with your statement of purpose. Your statement of purpose is a sacredly dedicated announcement to you, the power within; to you, the power below; to others; and to the creative Power on High. It declares who you are, what you do, and what you get as a result of who you are and what you do.

After you complete your purpose statement, begin to link each of the seven areas of life to your purpose with declarative statements. The seven areas of life are spiritual, mental, physical, financial, familial, career, and social.

Realize that a purpose statement that rambles on is a sure sign of distractions. I will not tell you exactly *how* long is too long. Just ask yourself, Does every word have a purpose? Also, realize that too many affirmations will be too much for you to begin to take action on. Prioritize your affirmations. Have many goals but link them to your few affirmations. Between one and five affirmations for each of the seven areas of life is a wise choice. I will not tell you exactly how many affirmations for each area is right for you. You know. Less than one or more than five is probably a sign of distraction. Your total number of affirmations for the seven areas of your life should be 7 or more, and less than 25.

I invite you to complete the following statements in your mind for each of your seven areas of life. The following are examples of how you can word your affirmations.

✦ "I am as focused as a laser point of light on my purpose" (being), or

✦ "You are as focused as a laser point of light on your purpose" (being).

✦ "I am breathing deeply and powerfully daily" (doing), or

✦ "You are breathing deeply and powerfully daily" (doing).

✦ "I am experiencing gratitude and inspiration daily" (having), or

✦ "You are experiencing gratitude and inspiration daily" (having).

Both forms of affirmations—"I am" and "you are" (being, doing, having)—are useful.

Affirmations help us to accelerate our evolution in time and space by increasing our vibration of thought and expanding our conscious awareness. Affirmations cause us to more quickly evolve from unconsciously unconscious to superconsciously superconscious. The diameter up the spiral staircase becomes smaller and smaller while the rate of vertical ascent becomes faster and faster.

Suppose you were to make the following questions your deepest, innermost, dominant, daily thought:

What am I thinking, visualizing, affirming, feeling, and acting on to make what I love to be, do, and have come into form? And how does it serve my purpose?

Imagine what would happen if you were to consistently hold your thought on your vision, aligned with your purpose, to where you naturally find yourself in the right place at the right time, meeting the right people, encountering the right events, thinking the right thoughts that birth the right ideas. Imagine the gratitude and inspiration you experience as you continue to purposely focus, imagine, affirm, feel, and act more deeply, to the point that the right people, places, ideas, and events mysteriously blend to a point of perfect synthesis that makes your dreams come true.

You have a choice. You may not feel the need to decide to affirm what you love to be, do, and have now, but if you did have the courage to ferociously affirm and immediately act on your dreams, how surprised would you be to suddenly discover that you begin to truly realize a whole new world of possibilities, as the perfect new people, places, ideas, and events appear to assist you on your mission?

May the creature about you succumb to the force of the creative designer within you now. I invite you to begin to design your life today by applying purposeful, focused thought on your vision, with affirmation, to the point that infatuations and resentments fall away as the intangible truth of symmetrical love beyond time and space (your why or cause) for your creation is birthed, giving birth to the tangible (how or effect) in time and space, beginning now.

What we resist persists.

What we fear draws near.

What we have guilt about
is rebuilt about us.

What we resent is re-sent.

What we run from we run into.

What we bury buries us.

What we repress will progress
and be expressed.

Our lies (exaggerations and minimizations)
will find us out.

5

FEELING

To feel, we perceive a non-localized physical sensation as we become aware of, touch, and find ourselves in the mood, burning with desire for the object of our laser-like focus of intention that is congruent with our mission. As you begin to get a crystal-clear understanding of feeling, notice the difference between (1) burning with desire for the object of your laser-like focus of intention that is congruent with your mission, and (2) an intense state of disturbance expressed by an excessive and theatrical manner. In other words, notice the difference between the One true feeling and the many emotions.

The word "emote," which is the root of emotion, means "to express feeling in an excessive or theatrical manner." The word "ion" means "an atom or molecule that is altered from its neutral, stable state by acquiring a net electrical charge by gaining or losing one or more electrons or charges." Aristotle said, "All men [and women] become easily deceived and more so the more their emotions are excited." You can begin to understand that emot*ions* are exaggerations and minimizations from the One true feeling (love) proportionate to the degree of net charge, either + or − charges. In the Gospel of Thomas, verse 22 states, "When you make the two one, and when you make the inner out of the outer and the outer as the inner, and the above as the below, and when you make the female into a single one, then you shall enter the Kingdom." Eventually you can naturally find yourself realizing that the one neutral $(+ = -)$, stable state is mysteriously and instantaneously felt at the point of synthesis where the polar opposite, abstract entities combine to birth a transformed, enlightened, unified, and relatively noble entity. These polar opposite, abstract entities are those of infatuation and resentment, exaggeration and minimization, fears of the future and guilts about the past. The transformed, enlightened, unified, and noble entity is love. Love is the one feeling that transcends time and space. Emotions dissipate as they scatter by dispersion toward the center to give rise to One true feeling that is the unifying force that births creation.

I consulted with a mother and daughter who had spent the last three years polarized against one another and not speaking to each other. The mother's sister had encouraged her to travel to Houston (from Colorado) and come to me for a consultation with her daughter in the hope of breaking through the impasse.

To help them rediscover their connection with each other, I worked with them to dissolve one illusive, emotionally charged resentment—or lopsided exaggeration or minimization—after another, until the light of unconditional love dawned on them.

After working with them from 7:00 p.m. until 1:00 a.m., they finally realized their love for each other and embraced with tears of love, gratitude, and inspiration. They have maintained an open-hearted communication since that night.

As you begin to understand the difference between emotions and the One true feeling of love, I invite you to realize that emotions are distorters that are neither good nor bad. As you continue to see clearly, the relevant question is: Does the dog wag the tail or does the tail wag the dog? When our emotions are the master over us, there is disordered chaos. When *we* run our emotions, there is ordered poise. To the degree that we are master of our emotions we can, through our power within, choose to be "in the world" of emotions, but not "of the world" of emotions. I invite you to allow yourself to realize that each frustum or layer of concentric rings of consciousness we transcend, by rising above and beyond them through love, gives expression to a greater intensity of power in our lives. By transcending a level of consciousness, we step out of being a manifested creature, and rise to the occasion of being a manifesting creator.

Our purpose gives us something greater than ourselves on which to focus our laser-like attention. The greater the magnitude of time and space that our purpose and thought transcends, the greater the vision. The greater the vision, the greater the love. The greater the degree and magnitude of love, the greater the force we generate to manifest what we love. Love is the glue that holds the universe together. Love is the alpha and the omega. Love is the force that transcends time and space.

Each moment in time will die and be reborn, yet love persists. The form may change, but the essence remains the same. Love is often hidden by our perceptions until we find the beauty in our perceived past and future moments now. Love appears to be both forward and backward in what we call time. As we look back on time, we realize that love appears in what we call the past. As we look forward in what we call time, we realize that love appears in what we call the future. You can realize that past love and future love are now. Love transcends past and future. Love unifies past and future to now. Past and future collapse inward to now. Now is the only point in time we ever had or ever will have. Love is now.

Love is present in whatever space we find ourselves. If we move from here to there, love is already there (or what we perceive to be there); and if we could move from there to here, love is already here (or what we perceive to be here). Love is present. Love unifies here and there such that there is here and here is there in present space, because love transcends what we call space. They collapse inward to present consciousness. Love transcends time and space to "present now." I invite you to consider that without language there would be no past or future, here or there—only present now.

Love is present now. By our senses we would judge that it waits patiently, yet actually it is beyond waiting in time and space. Love is symmetry, proportion, order, and precision to the relative magnitude that it is beyond the horizontal paradox of the bicameral senses of the power below and is present now in the vertical groove of the higher-minded unicameral power within. Love is present now in the vertical groove. Love is groovy! Love is a vertically groovy, cosmically inspired radio station that transmits its frequency from above, down, inside, and out.

If we fail to see the symmetrical beauty in our lives, we will tend to experience internally the lower-minded emotional feelings of depression, paranoia, meaninglessness, and addiction that are rooted in fear of the future and guilt about the past. Whatever is within us will tend to be around us, and whatever is around us will tend to be within us.

Whatever we resist persists. Whatever we fear draws near. Whatever we have guilt about is built about us. Whatever we resent is re-sent. Whatever we bury buries us. Whatever we run from we run into. Whatever we repress will progress and be expressed. Our lies (exaggerations and minimizations) will find us out. The form may change, but the essence remains the same.

The ancient Egyptian sage Amen-em-apt wrote, "Ask not why God allows evil to exist whilst thou thyself are doing thy utmost to stir up strife." If we do not know ourselves well and love what we know about ourselves, we will require much stimulation from outside ourselves to fill the perceived vacuum. We will seek excitement by way of exaggeration and minimization to keep us too busy to go deep inside and be honest. Before we can experience love, we must first experience the integration of all our parts and pieces (personas), leading us to a foundation of integrity.

Socrates said, "The unexamined life is not worth living." Realize that your self-worth grows in proportion to how closely you examine and find the beauty in your life. Discovering the beauty uncovers love.

With conscious awareness and action comes integrity. With integrity comes integration of our scattered parts and pieces into a unified whole. Love is the integrator. A foundation of integrity allows us to take responsibility for our life. To be responsible means to be able to choose how we respond. Between the level of unconsciously unconscious and superconsciously superconscious we are in varying degrees of being able to choose our response to life.

On one end of the continuum we take a positional, postulative stance as we perceive ourselves to be a victim of circumstance. We attract and move toward completing a circle of self-perpetuating events about our polar charge of our position to validate our illusional victimhood. We dis-integratively find ourselves creatively avoiding owning our own creations. We avoid being responsible by pendulum-shifting between not giving ourselves permission due to feeling unworthy, and feeling afraid and angry. We withhold permission to ourselves or feel unworthy out of guilt (a perception of more pain than pleasure) about the past. We feel anger out of a fear of gaining pain or losing pleasure in the future.

On the other end of the continuum we rise above the duality of the paradox. From our perspective on high we can clearly see that we are heroic co-creators of circumstances that are part of our journey. We attract and move toward our purpose with responsible integrity on the vertical plane and the horizontal axis. We accept both pleasure and pain in the horizontal axis as we move vertically with the pleasure of purpose that transcends pleasure and pain on the horizontal plane.

You can easily understand that fear and guilt may serve a purpose of preserving your form in order to allow the power within you to fulfill its mission aligned with the Power from on High. A rational fear system can cause us to react instantaneously and ferociously to defend ourselves or flee from others. A rational guilt system will cause us to react instantaneously to a powerful perception of pain and immediately stop and align our actions with something higher than the power below. Beyond the primitive functions of fight or flight and immediate alignment with one or more persons, places, ideas, or events greater than ourselves, fear and guilt are not necessary on the vertical path of the heart.

Perhaps now you can see that fear and guilt—cloaked in feelings of anger, unworthiness, worry, and other emotions—are subtle, disintegrative prayers that tune us to the wavefront of people, places, ideas, or events that validate our feelings of anger, unworthiness, worry, and other emotions as a self-fulfilling and replicating prophecy. As you continue to clearly perceive that what we predominantly think about, envision, affirm in our language, and feel is what we become, move toward, and attract, consider that we exaggerate and minimize in order to justify and defend the lethargically complacent, self-serving, and cozy positional personas that distract our focus of attention from what we love to be, do, and have.

We exaggerate and defend our position by projecting our fears and guilts onto others to avoid coming to a point of honest balance in which we can stop and clearly see the symmetrically perfect benefit to self and others. We exaggerate and minimize the truth of the past (an asymmetrical perception of remembered greater pain or reduced pleasure) and the future (an asymmetrical perception of imagined greater future pain or reduced future pleasure).

Have you ever considered that to be, do, and have what we love, we must love who we are, what we do, and what we have? As you begin to truly love who you are as you are now, what you do now, and what you have now, your gratitude allows you to immediately begin to truly *design* who you are, what you do, and what you have, with total love, passionate purpose, and infinite detail.

Creators manifest in realms of consciousness that they have transcended by understanding and appreciating. Creators envision greater magnitudes of time and space. Creators feel love for all that exists within magnitudes of time and space they have transcended.

Creatures manifest in realms of consciousness that they do not understand and appreciate. Creatures envision lesser magnitudes of time and space. Creatures feel infatuations and resentments, and fear and guilt for and about what exists in lesser magnitudes of time and space that they have not transcended with love.

For example, suppose a person from a small town had traveled extensively, and understood and appreciated people and cultures around the world (space); and suppose this person had studied history and imagined the future in great visual detail (time). Now suppose another person had rarely left the same town and had never left the region. He or she had not studied history or imagined the future beyond today. Which one would feel more freedom to create their destiny? Which would feel more constricted and created by destiny? Would you agree that the person with greater understanding, appreciation, vision, and love would feel more freedom to create their destiny? Would you agree that the person with little or no understanding, appreciation, vision, and love for time and space beyond their existence would feel more constricted and created by destiny?

The greater the magnitude of understanding and love, the greater the magnitude of intelligence from the Power on High we tune to. The greater the power, the greater the magnetic, conscious force we generate to interact with matter. Matter without spirit is motionless to our perception. I invite you to consider that matter and spirit are present now beyond our senses. The degree to which we transcend here and there, then past and then future, by collapsing the dichotomies into a unified present now, is proportionate to the degree we link up with the Power on High and discover ourselves raised aloft to the majestically noble and sublime throne of co-creation.

Suppose you were to find yourself present now and assuming the functioning role of co-creator. How surprised would you be to naturally discover that a universal law put into motion can be readily perceived by a creature as a mysteriously incredible "miracle," and that same incredible miracle is perceived by a creator as a natural and infinite expression of universal law? You can easily allow yourself to continue to act as a loving creator and designer of your life now, as you know your purpose, and you know deep within you that you know that you know. Follow your purpose with focused concentration of thought to such a degree that you experience colorful and detailed vision, and you hear the crystal-clear voice of the Power on High speak its affirming and inspiring message through your heart. Your heart opens and expands to embrace both sides of contradiction and paradox, carrying you to a higher level of being, doing, and having now. Imagine what it would feel like if your love and gratitude added power to your affirmative words, and hold your vision with focused thought on your purpose.

You have a choice. You may not want to begin to assume the functioning role as co-creator now. But if you stop and consider the alternative role as creature on the horizontal plane, you can clearly see that the vertical path of purpose, thought, vision, affirmation, and the One true feeling of love transcending pain and pleasure is truly of the highest order. Notice what it is like when you, the higher-minded power within, purposefully link up with the Power on High. As you direct and guide the power below with authority from on high, such that it listens and acts through your sensory and motor system in symmetrical and unified accordance with the divine chain of command flowing from above, down, inside, and out.

As you continue to purposefully focus on your vision while affirming your inspirational words of power, you can begin to become aware of the incredible feeling flowing through you like electricity! As you feel that feeling, you find yourself becoming aware of hearing a single, subtle, sustained tone. The sound begins to amplify the incredible feeling flowing through you now. As the soft, subtle, sublime tone vibrates, and that incredible electrical feeling intensifies, you might see yourself experiencing

what you purposefully love to be, do, and have while you imagine yourself immediately beginning to perceive your innermost,
dominant loves in each area of your life now.

I invite you to continue to conceive with purposeful detail
the person, place, idea, or event with which your heart lovingly
resonates. As you continue to resonate with that which your
love mysteriously attracts, you instantly envision a brilliant picture in infinite detail on the movie screen of your mind. You
can form the essence of your unlimited vision into a brilliantly
colored, rotating sphere. As your love for your created vision
holds your crystal-clear image, and you feel the sublime tone
vibrating through your inner power within, while you listen
with great attention to the gentle humming, single tone of resonating frequency emanating from your sphere, what color is
your sphere, and does it spin to the left or right or both? As you
find yourself attracting the sphere to you and hold your creation
in your hand so gently with love, you can begin to breathe the
breath of life into your intangible creation by uniting love and
gratitude with the tangible step of writing your vision in form,
in space and time, and taking action with energy now.

Writing is the first step in the transformation of our intangible love to the tangible form.

6
WRITING

Have you ever considered that writing is clearly the most fundamental action step to begin manifesting what you would love to be, do, and have? Would you start on a journey to a faraway land without a map? Would you continue your journey without considering your coordinates in time and space? Would you build a complex structured form without a blueprint? Would you build this form without adjusting your design to make it more ergonomic and aerodynamic?

To manifest what you would love to be, do, and have, you must know what you would love to be, do, and have. You can become, perform, and obtain what you love as you realize that you know what you love, align it with your purpose, focus your thought, hold your vision of it in infinite detail, and plot it in time and space.

Writing is the first step in transforming our intangible love to a tangible form. As we focus our thought on our vision, affirm it, and hold it to us with our love that we have birthed in our relatively formless and intangible memory and imagination, we can begin to bring to life who and what we love. We do this through effective planning, by characterizing with angular form in spatial coordinates on the horizontal plane, and continuing to maintain our present-now consciousness in the continuum of what we call time and space.

Have you ever considered that writing in time and space can lead us, the higher-minded power within, to transform our emotional charge for what we fear, have guilt about, resent, bury, run from and repress? Have the courage to discover the truth of precise symmetry, proportion, and order in what you fear, have guilt about, resent, bury, run from, and repress. You can suddenly find yourself rising above the paradoxes of fear and guilt, infatuation and resentment, exaggeration and minimization, omission and commission, and being born anew in the golden realm of co-creation. I invite you to understand that until you finally and truly see the even-sided beauty of all that has gone before, you cannot be present now with who you are, what you do, and what you have. And you cannot feel free to focus, with present-now consciousness, on what you would love to have in your future. Writing is a means to perceiving even-sided beauty and infinite clarity.

As you go deep inside your heart now, via your mind, you can allow yourself to become aware of the people and events that push your buttons. Who and what are they? List your button pushers now.

_____

_____

_____

_____

_____

Which one of your button pushers pushes your buttons the most? Write the name of the one person or event that pushes your buttons the most now.

_____

What are the characteristics of your biggest button pusher that push your buttons the most?

_____

_____

_____

_____

_____

Which of these characteristics pushes your buttons the most?

_____

Have you ever considered that in order to recognize something in another person you must have the essence of that aspect within yourself? We can only recognize what we truly have a history of, and we judge others for what we do not accept in ourselves. Can you imagine the energy we expend in order to hold our position?

Now imagine yourself delving deeply inside your mind and heart to that centered point between excess and deficiency. You might find yourself becoming aware that your biggest button pusher—and the biggest button he, she, or it pushes—dissolves as you instantaneously discover the symmetrical, proportionate counterbalance and realize that you too have performed the same action or had the same thought in equal degree, magnitude, and amplitude to the charge you hold.

How surprised would you be to suddenly discover self as other? Imagine the feeling of release as you list the blessings of what you have judged for so long. List the blessings you have received from your biggest button pusher now.

_____

_____

_____

_____

_____

_____

_____

Suppose you were to write the pros (infatuations) (+) and cons (resentments) (−) of your biggest button pusher in infinite detail for 220 episodes each, now. Imagine what it would feel like to finally become aware that you have lived each of those pros and each of those cons somewhere in your life, equal in degree, kind, magnitude, multitude, quantity, and quality. The form may have changed, but the essence remains the same, somewhere in the seven areas of your life, past or present.

In the appendix at the end of this book you will find 20 communication enhancement forms, designed to help you dissolve your lopsided emotional charge on your one biggest button pusher. It's important that you choose only one person, place, idea, or event to work on at a time. You may need to use all 20 forms before you feel complete with the process. Or you may feel complete with slightly fewer pages. You will know you have completed this process when you begin to feel unconditional love and gratitude for this person, and you might find yourself experiencing non-local communication with them. You might experience "happy tears" or tears of inspiration. I can't tell you when you are complete with this process. However, you will know that you know. And I assure you if you will work the process it will work for you. An example is also included to help get you started.

I invite you to readily begin to dissolve your polar charges (+ or −) of your biggest button pusher toward unity (+ = −) now. Turn to the first communication enhancement form in the appendix. After you have listed, with symmetry, the pros and cons in columns 1 and 3 , you can begin to see the proportion, order, and beauty; and complete columns 2 and 4 as you find the pros and cons in yourself. It is important that you complete columns 1 and 3 before you move on to columns 2 and 4; the exercise is much easier to complete in this sequence.

Please do not underestimate the power of this exercise! If you will take the time to complete all 20 forms, you will experience amazing and magical transformations in your life.

✛ ✛ ✛

When you have completed the communication enhancement forms, you can begin to understand that when we clear our lower-minded emotions, stored in the lower-minded power below, we can begin to experience a new universe of possibilities as we find ourselves beginning to think about, feel about, and see things in a whole new way. As you continue to see things in a new way, realize that the previous writing exercise, called a "collapse," is a way to unite the power below with the power within, and the power within with the Power on High, establishing a divine chain of command from above, down, inside, and out.

Can you imagine the incredible changes that would occur in your life if you were to do a collapse process on 12 people, places, ideas, or events that push your buttons now? Suppose you were to do a collapse process on 49 people, places, ideas, or events that push your buttons now. Imagine the powerful transformation that would occur if you were to do a collapse process on 144 people, places, ideas, or events. Realize that the more we collapse our emotional charge toward the center of the zero-point of love, the greater our influence on the people, places, ideas, and events that manifest in our lives. We are transformed within from victim to victor.

Suppose you were able to instantaneously see — in your mind and heart — the symmetry, proportion, and order in any person, place, idea, or event that pushes your buttons. You could go deep inside your mind and heart and ask yourself:

+ Where have I done this equally in magnitude and multitude?

+ In what area of life did I do it?

+ How has this person, place, idea, or event helped me?

+ In which of the seven areas of life did he, she, or it help me?

+ Did he, she, or it help me *spiritually* to become closer to my true nature?

+ Did he, she, or it help me *mentally* to be more intelligent, determined, and focused?

+ Did he, she, or it help me *physically* to become stronger, healthier, or better able to withstand events that occurred later?

- Did he, she, or it help me *socially* to excel in my community, or help me to expand the size of community in which I interact?

- Did he, she, or it help me in my *family* relationships to be closer and with greater love?

- Did he, she, or it help me in my *career* to rise to new heights of production and accomplishment?

- Did he, she, or it help me in my *finances* to be wiser in saving and spending?

The collapse process was developed by Dr. John F. Demartini of the Concourse of Wisdom School of Healing and Philosophy. I am grateful to him for sharing this "science of love" with me, and allowing me to reprint the communication enhancement form, also known as a "collapse form."

If you have not yet completed all 20 communication enhancement forms, I encourage you to go back and do so now. You do not have to complete the collapse forms now, but if you were to begin immediately, how surprised would you be to find yourself gaining the inner, peaceful wisdom of a wise elder, without having to age to get the understanding and gratitude?

You will collapse your emotional charges as you proceed through the time and space of your life. Your Power on High will allow you the power within to experience enough pain (from listening to the lower-minded power below) to force you to humble yourself to the Power on High and guide you back to a perception of beauty, leading you to acceptance, gratitude, and unconditional love for what is, as it is.

✦ Each individual infatuation or resentment to which we bring the light of symmetry, proportion, order, precision, and gratitude is like removing one leaf from a twig.

✦ Each complete line of infatuation and resentment to which we bring the light of truth is like removing one twig.

✦ Each person, place, idea, or event for which we collapse our charge, and for which we find symmetry, proportion, order, precision, and gratitude is like removing a branch to find the noonday sun shining through, warming our heart with evermore inspiration as we remove branch after branch with each successive collapse.

The process of completing the communication enhancement forms allows you to accelerate your transformational evolution of your life now. I encourage you to know that you have the infinite courage and wisdom to continue to use the collapse process daily.

✦ ✦ ✦

As we begin to allow ourselves to look back on our life with incredibly perceptive understanding, we can easily see the divinely magnificent, infinitely perfect design in what we perceived to be voids in our past. These "voids" guided us toward our ultimate purpose in this life.

Imagine knowing that you could not fail, and that nothing could stop you from becoming, creating, and owning who you would love to be and what you would love to do and have.

- ✦ Who would you be, and what would you do and have?

- ✦ What would be the most important actions you would take to have an immortal effect in time and space?

- ✦ What would someone who knew the "real you" write for your epitaph?

- ✦ What would your life be like if you acted as if today was both your last and best day?

- ✦ What would you do if today was the first day of the rest of your life?

Write the top 49 things you would love to become, perform, or obtain in the next year. See these goals as red. (You may want to use colored markers through this exercise.)

1. _____

2. _____

3. _____

4. _____

5. _____

6. _____

7. _____

8. _____

9. _____

10. _____

11. _____

12. _____

13. _____

14. _____

15. _____

16. _____

17. _____

18. _____

19. _____

20. _____

21. _____

22. _____

23. _____

24. _____

25. _____

26. _____

27. _____

28. _____

29. _____

30. _____

31. _____

32. _____

33. _____

34. _____

35. _____

36. _____

37. _____

38. _____

39. _____

40. _____

41. _____

42. _____

43. _____

44. _____

45. _____

46. _____

47. _____

48. _____

49. _____

Write the top 33 things you would love to become, perform, or obtain in the next five years. See these goals as orange.

1. _____

2. _____

3. _____

4. _____

5. _____

6. _____

7. _____

8. _____

9. _____

10. _____

11. _____

12. _____

13. _____

14. _____

15. _____

16. _____

17. _____

18. _____

19. _____

20. _____

21. _____

22. _____

23. _____

24. _____

25. _____

26. _____

27. _____

28. _____

29. _____

30. _____

31. _____

32. _____

33. _____

Write the top 12 things you would love to become, perform, or obtain in the next ten years. See these goals as yellow.

1. _____

2. _____

3. _____

4. _____

5. _____

6. _____

7. _____

8. _____

9. _____

10. _____

11. _____

12. _____

Write the top 9 things you would love to become, perform, or obtain in the next twenty years. See these goals as green.

1. _____

2. _____

3. _____

4. _____

5. _____

6. _____

7. _____

8. _____

9. _____

Write the top 7 things you would love to become, perform, or obtain in the next thirty years. See these goals as blue.

1. _____

2. _____

3. _____

4. _____

5. _____

6. _____

7. _____

Write the top 5 things you would love to become, perform, or obtain in the next forty years. See these goals as indigo.

1. _____

2. _____

3. _____

4. _____

5. _____

Write the top 3 goals you would love to become, perform, or obtain for this lifetime. See these goals as violet.

1. _____

2. _____

3. _____

✳ ✳ ✳

Imagine that you are at the end of a long life. What is the one purposeful, immortal effect you would love to leave for your neighbors in time and space?

Write the #1 purposeful, immortal effect you would love to leave behind in time and space after you leave your physical form. (See this goal as white.)

White goal _____

_____

_____

_____

_____

_____

_____

_____

_____

Those goals that are less aligned vertically to your purposeful immortal effect are only distractions along the way. The greater the horizontal angle of perpendicularity to your purpose, the greater the distractive self-infatuation and self-resentment cycles. The smaller the horizontal angle of perpendicularity to your purpose, the greater the self-appreciation you repeatedly experience as you find yourself focusing with microscopic detail on your purpose, like a laser point of light.

Now that you have determined your #1 purposeful, immortal effect you would love to leave behind, look back on your violet, indigo, blue, green, yellow, orange, and red goals and ask yourself if they all integrate well with your #1 purposeful, immortal effect. You now have an opportunity to fine tune your goals.

Write your top 3 goals for your lifetime.

(See these goals as violet.)

Violet goal #1 _____

Violet goal #2 _____

Violet goal #3 _____

Now compare your violet goals to your white, purposeful, immortal effect. Assign a priority of "1" to the violet goal that aligns and links most closely with your white, purposeful, immortal effect. Assign a priority of "2" to the goal that aligns the second most closely with your purposeful, immortal effect. Assign a priority of "3" to the goal that aligns the third most closely with your purposeful, immortal effect. If any goal does not align with and support your one immortal effect, circle it and mark next to it a capital T for "tangent." Feel free to substitute another goal that aligns with and supports your superior, higher-ordered purpose. After you have completed this process, move to the next set of goals.

Write your top 5 goals for the next forty years.
(See these goals as indigo.)

Indigo goal #1 _____

Indigo goal #2 _____

Indigo goal #3 _____

Indigo goal #4 _____

Indigo goal #5 _____

Compare your indigo goals to your one, white, purposeful, immortal effect and your 3 violet goals. Now assign priorities from "1" through "5" according to how closely each one aligns with and supports the one, white, immortal effect and the 3 violet goals. If any goal does not align with and support your one immortal effect or 3 violet goals, circle it and mark next to it a capital T for "tangent." Feel free to substitute another goal that aligns with and supports your superior, higher-ordered purpose. After you've completed this process, move to the next set of goals.

Write your top 7 goals for the next thirty years.
(See these goals as blue.)

Blue goal #1 _____

Blue goal #2 _____

Blue goal #3 _____

Blue goal #4 _____

Blue goal #5 _____

Blue goal #6 _____

Blue goal #7 _____

Compare your blue goals to your one, white, purposeful, immortal effect, your 3 violet goals, and your 5 indigo goals. Assign priorities from "1" through "7" according to how closely each one aligns with your one, white, immortal effect and your supporting goals. If any goal does not align with and support your one immortal effect or supporting goals, circle it and mark next to it a capital T for "tangent." Feel free to substitute another goal that aligns with and supports your superior, higher-ordered purpose. After you have completed this process, move to the next set of goals.

Write your top 9 goals for the next twenty years.
(See these goals as green.)

Green goal #1 _____

Green goal #2 _____

Green goal #3 _____

Green goal #4 _____

Green goal #5 _____

Green goal #6 _____

Green goal #7 _____

Green goal #8 _____

Green goal #9 _____

Now compare your green goals to your one, white, purposeful, immortal effect, your 3 violet goals, your 5 indigo goals, and your 7 blue goals. Assign priorities from "1" through "9" according to how closely each one aligns with your one, white, immortal effect and your supporting goals. If any goal does not align with and support your one, white, immortal effect or supporting goals, circle it and mark next to it a capital T for "tangent." Feel free to substitute another goal that aligns with and supports your superior, higher-ordered purpose. After you have completed this process, move to the next set of goals.

Write your top 12 goals for the next ten years.
(See these goals as yellow.)

Yellow goal #1 _____

Yellow goal #2 _____

Yellow goal #3 _____

Yellow goal #4 _____

Yellow goal #5 _____

Yellow goal #6 _____

Yellow goal #7 _____

Yellow goal #8 _____

Yellow goal #9 _____

Yellow goal #10 _____

Yellow goal #11 _____

Yellow goal #12 _____

Now compare your yellow goals to your one, white, purposeful, immortal effect, your 3 violet goals, your 5 indigo goals, your 7 blue goals, and your 9 green goals. Assign priorities from "1" through "12" according to how closely each one aligns with your one, white, immortal effect and your supporting goals. If any goal does not align with and support your one, white, purposeful, immortal effect or supporting goals, circle it and mark next to it a capital T for "tangent." Feel free to substitute another goal that aligns with and supports your superior, higher-ordered purpose. After you have completed this process, move to the next set of goals.

Write your top 33 goals for the next five years.
(See these goals as orange.)

Orange goal #1 _____

Orange goal #2 _____

Orange goal #3 _____

Orange goal #4 _____

Orange goal #5 _____

Orange goal #6 _____

Orange goal #7 _____

Orange goal #8 _____

Orange goal #9 _____

Orange goal #10 _____

Orange goal #11 _____

Orange goal #12 _____

Orange goal #13 _____

Orange goal #14 _____

Orange goal #15 _____

Orange goal #16 _____

Orange goal #17 _____

Orange goal #18 _____

Orange goal #19 _____

Orange goal #20 _____

Orange goal #21 _____

Orange goal #22 _____

Orange goal #23 _____

Orange goal #24 _____

Orange goal #25 _____

Orange goal #26 _____

Orange goal #27 _____

Orange goal #28 _____

Orange goal #29 _____

Orange goal #30 _____

Orange goal #31 _____

Orange goal #32 _____

Orange goal #33 _____

Compare your orange goals to your one, white, purposeful, immortal effect, your 3 violet goals, your 5 indigo goals, your 7 blue goals, your 9 green goals, and your 12 yellow goals. Assign priorities from "1" through "33" according to how closely each one aligns with your one, white, immortal effect and your supporting goals. If any goal does not align with and support your one, purposeful, immortal effect or supporting goals, circle it and mark next to it a capital T for "tangent." Feel free to substitute another goal that aligns with and supports your superior, higher-ordered purpose. After you have completed this process, move to the next set of goals.

Write your top 49 goals for the next year.

(See these goals as red.)

Red goal #1 _____

Red goal #2 _____

Red goal #3 _____

Red goal #4 _____

Red goal #5 _____

Red goal #6 _____

Red goal #7 _____

Red goal #8 _____

Red goal #9 _____

Red goal #10 _____

Red goal #11 _____

Red goal #12 _____

Red goal #13 _____

Red goal #14 _____

Red goal #15 _____

Red goal #16 _____

Red goal #17 _____

Red goal #18 _____

Red goal #19 _____

Red goal #20 _____

Red goal #21 _____

Red goal #22 _____

Red goal #23 _____

Red goal #24 _____

Red goal #25 _____

Red goal #26 _____

Red goal #27 _____

Red goal #28 _____

Red goal #29 _____

Red goal #30 _____

Red goal #31 _____

Red goal #32 _____

Red goal #33 _____

Red goal #34 _____

Red goal #35 _____

Red goal #36 _____

Red goal #37 _____

Red goal #38 _____

Red goal #39 _____

Red goal #40 _____

Red goal #41 _____

Red goal #42 _____

Red goal #43 _____

Red goal #44 _____

Red goal #45 _____

Red goal #46 _____

Red goal #47 _____

Red goal #48 _____

Red goal #49 _____

Compare your red goals to your one, white, purposeful, immortal effect, your 3 violet goals, your 5 indigo goals, your 7 blue goals, your 9 green goals, your 12 yellow goals, and your 33 orange goals. Assign priorities from "1" through "49" to each of your one-year goals according to how closely each aligns with your one, white, immortal effect and your supporting goals. If any goal does not align with and support your one, purposeful, immortal effect or supporting goals, circle it and mark next to it a capital T for "tangent." Feel free to substitute another goal that aligns with and supports your superior, higher-ordered purpose.

The next step is to connect the lists by color. You might find yourself discovering new insights as you look upon your beautifully detailed creation. Count the number of your 49 red goals that align with and support your one white, purposeful, immortal effect. Then count the number of red goals that align with and support your violet goals. Repeat this process for your indigo goals, blue goals, green goals, yellow goals, and orange goals, in that order. Write the number of each of the higher-ordered colors that your red goals align with and support.

Now repeat this process—ascending up the color spectrum—for your orange goals, yellow goals, green goals, blue goals, indigo goals, and violet goals.

✦ I invite you to consider that the greater the number of

your 49 red goals that resonate with your one immortal effect, the greater the certainty of actualization. The greater the number of red goals that resonate with your violet goals, the greater the certainty; and so on for your indigo, blue, green, yellow, and orange goals, respectively.

✦ A similar hierarchy applies to your 33 orange goals, beginning with your one immortal effect and descending through the 12 yellow goals.

✦ A similar hierarchy applies to your 12 yellow goals, beginning with your one immortal effect and descending through your 9 green goals.

✦ And so on for your 7 blue, 5 indigo, and 3 violet goals.

Before continuing, I ask you now to read pages 141 and 142, and then return to this page.

Imagine yourself standing with your hands at your sides, palms open and facing forward. Notice what it feels like when you raise your head and eyes upward and close your eyes gently. As you continue to stand upright in inspiration, begin to think about and feel appreciation for the people, events, and places that have truly blessed you in your life. While you ponder with gratitude the blessings of these experiences, you can express your gratitude to the people, events, and places and your Power on High for the values that you hold dear by opening your heart now. You might find yourself opening your heart and mind to your inspiring mission from on High.

Imagine what it would feel like if you were to simultaneously remember and imagine—with present-now consciousness— who you are, where you came from, where you are going, and why you are here now, to such a degree of certainty that you begin to hear a loving, parental voice speaking to you like a father or mother would speak to a son or daughter.

As you begin to see your vision and hear your calling from this Parent on High, you can feel its subtle force, like an inspiring stream flowing through you and out of you, and you experience tears of inspiration and gratitude for your message. After you receive your message about your purpose, you would be wise to immediately write it down. Below is a space for you to write your purpose statement now.

I _____ , the power within my physical form, do earnestly declare before myself, others, and the Perfect, Omnipotent, Omniscient Originator and Ruler of the Universe that my primary purpose is to:

_____

_____

_____

_____

_____

_____

_____

_____

_____

_____

Now that you have completed your purpose statement, you can begin to ponder your tangible goals. What would you love to be, do, and have in each area of your life?

+ How and who would you love to *be* physically?

+ How and who would you love to *be* mentally?

+ How and who would you love to *be* in your career?

+ How and who would you love to *be* in your finances?

+ How and who would you love to *be* socially?

+ How and who would you love to *be* in your relationships?

+ How and who would you love to *be* spiritually?

+ What would you love to *do* physically?

+ What would you love to *do* mentally?

+ What would you love to *do* as your vocation? What do you feel called to do?

+ What would you love to *do* financially?

+ What would you love to *do* socially?

+ What would you love to *do* in your family relationships?

+ What would you love to *do* spiritually?

+ What would you love to *have* physically?

+ What would you love to *have* mentally?

+ What would you love to *have* in your career?

+ What would you love to *have* financially?

+ What would you love to *have* socially?

✦ What would you love to *have* in your relationships?

✦ What would you love to *have* spiritually?

How are your goals aligned and linked to your purpose? Goals that are not aligned and linked with your purpose are relatively more transient, and fall like leaves from a tree. What are you willing to be, do, and have in order to be, do, and have what you love?

Are you ready and willing to cross to the center of the horizontal plane of pain and pleasure to move higher on your vertical path of your purpose, as you take greater action steps to what you truly love? Are you ready and willing to continue to totally dissolve your lower-minded, reactive emotional charges? As you ponder these questions, you may want to review your purpose statement.

You can write what you love in each area of your life now. Imagine what it would feel like if you were to find yourself being, doing, and having the events, actions, and things that you love most. As you feel the love for the events, actions, and things that align with your innermost, dominant thought, focused on your purpose, manifesting in time and space, you can conceive your love list. What is the highest priority (what you would love to be, do, and have) in each area of your life? Write your love list now.

"Be, Do, Have" Love List

Physical

Be _____

Do _____

Have _____

Mental

Be _____

Do _____

Have _____

Career

Be _____

Do _____

Have _____

Financial

Be _____

Do _____

Have _____

Social

Be _____

Do _____

Have _____

Family

Be _____

Do _____

Have _____

Spiritual

Be _____

Do _____

Have _____

Now that you have completed your love list, you can begin to design your affirmative words of power. You can readily use your be, do, and have love list as the raw material for processing and transforming into your words of power. I invite you to realize that brevity and intensity create brilliant immensity of conviction. Create a more powerful and higher-ordered affirmation by ensuring that each word has a goal linked to your purpose. Write your affirmations in the first person (I am) or second person (you are). Both are useful. Write your words of power now.

Words of Power

1. _____

2. _____

3. _____

4. _____

5. _____

6. _____

7. _____

8. _____

9. _____

10. _____

11. _____

12. _____

13. _____

14. _____

15. _____

16. _____

17. _____

18. _____

19. _____

20. _____

21. _____

22. _____

23. _____

24. _____

25. _____

Eventually you can understand that however your creation turned out is perfect for you. Notice where you are now. I recommend that you frequently write your hierarchical levels of goals aligned with and linked to your purpose. Each time you focus your energy and concentration, you enhance your faculties of perception and action to be, do, and have. Feel free to repeat the process as often as you feel it brings clarity and order to your mission of purpose.

I encourage you to have the infinite courage and wisdom to write your words of power daily and read your words of power morning, noon, and night. As you write and read your words of power daily, how surprised would you be to find yourself experiencing purposefully clear thought, incredibly detailed vision, affirmative words, and true, uncharged love for what you love to be, do, and have? I invite you to understand that removing and rewording your words of power is a sure sign of evolutionary progress. When self-doubt arises, get your words of power. Read your words of power out loud to yourself and read them with conviction. Hold your words of power up high and read with a conviction of certainty in your voice until you feel your state change.

Choose your friends wisely and carefully. Associate with people who are being, doing, and having some of what you love to be, do, and have; yet do not discuss your method of accomplishing what you love to be, do, and have with anyone but the Power on High. The Power on High does not enter into any controversial arguments. It is neither for nor against what you say you want. It is waiting and willing to serve you when your instinct knows that your mind knows that your heart knows that you love what you say you love. I invite you to be definite. Add detail. To the degree you can know that you know that you love it—with faith, confidence, certainty, and detail—is the degree you can realize your heart's desire.

Have you ever considered that if you cannot decide to write what you love, you are not in earnest? If you are not in earnest, you are not allowing yourself permission to give and receive what you love. If you are not allowing yourself permission, you are ultimately fearful of the future or feeling guilt about the past. Fear and guilt keep us trapped in a self-perpetuating life of quiet desperation. Why not live a life of incredibly purposeful and bold inspiration now?

Focusing on what we love, linked to our purpose through writing, leads us on the straightaway superhighway, instead of the tributaries of tangential dead ends and long-way-arounds we impose on ourselves when we listen to the future fears and past guilts of the power below. I invite you to realize that writing our loves is the first step in bringing our intangible visions, callings, and inspirations into three-dimensional, manifested form in time and space, while dissolving fear of the future in the process. Similarly, writing our infatuations and resentments in time and space helps us dissolve our emotionally charged exaggerations and minimizations of what is, transcending guilt about the past as we discover the symmetry, proportion, order, and precision with gratitude. As we dissolve our past guilts, we unravel our future fears. As we dissolve our future fears, we dissolve our past guilts.

I encourage you to continue to write your purpose statement, words of power, and your hierarchically termed purposeful goals while you continue to collapse your illusions daily. If you were to continue to write what you love in time and space, as you dissolve what you infatuate and resent by writing in time and space, how surprised would you be to find yourself feeling ever higher and higher levels of freedom to take action with energy now?

"Whatever you can do,
or dream you can ... begin it.
Boldness has genius, power,
and magic in it."

– Goethe

7

ACTION

We were excitedly standing outside the side entrance to the Semiramis Hotel in Cairo. It was around 10:30 p.m. After what seemed like a long time an Egyptian man appeared. He informed us that we could not get into the King's Chamber, but that he could get us to the Great Pyramid. He would arrange with a guard to let us climb to the top of the pyramid—something I had expressed a desire to do before I had left Houston. There was a certain degree of risk involved beyond the obvious risk of bodily injury and intense physical demand: it was forbidden to climb the pyramid.

Earlier that day the Egyptian man had approached us at the Sphinx and told us that he could get us inside at night. We were interested in getting into the King's Chamber of the Great Pyramid at night, when we would be undisturbed by other tourists. This enterprising man told us that for $150 (U.S.) he would pay certain guards to look the other way as we made our way to the pyramid and scaled its face. Fifteen of us agreed to his proposal, accepting the inherent risk involved in achieving what we knew we would love to do.

We gathered that evening and waited to be transported to the starting point of our truly incredible adventure. We piled into a tiny minivan and began our mysterious, exciting journey. We talked and joked among ourselves as we traveled to our destination. We stopped once along the way to pick up an Egyptian man. After about forty minutes we arrived at a residential area and stopped at its northwest corner next to a huge lot of sand. As we entered the lot, the stench of camel urine filled the air.

The guide led us through the desert sand and up a hill, then down a valley into a graveyard. We negotiated our way in the darkness. Any form of light was strictly forbidden, to prevent being spotted by the pyramid guards. Our guide had told us that if we were caught, we were to deny that anyone had brought us in. We made our way through the graveyard and encountered more sand.

After walking over another sand dune we came to a place where we could see the southern side of the pyramids. We continued until we reached an area of ruins about two hundred yards from the Great Pyramid. We hid in the shadows and rested for about ten minutes. We briefly met a friendly man wearing a turban who was quickly gone. I noticed the stars and a crescent moon shining brightly—unlike any I had ever seen. One member of our group sprained her ankle and was unable to continue.

Our guide led us to the edge of the ruins. There he explained that we would go in groups of five. I made sure I jockeyed for position to be in the first group to climb. We were told that we would be met at the pyramid by an elderly man with a turban, and that he would help us.

The guide gave my group the signal to go and we took off at a trot across the sand, moving side by side in the night. We crossed an area roughly the length of a football field to reach the pyramid. At some point along the way we heard someone to our left shouting angrily in Arabic. I felt a surge of adrenaline as we broke into a sprint. During the run I suddenly felt the firmness of a dirt road under my feet, and then sand once again.

Shortly after we crossed the road we encountered the elderly man in a turban; he was waiting for us in the shadows close to the pyramid. He led us to the southwest edge of the Great Pyramid. He told us to stay at the corner as we climbed. It made sense to me that we would be less visible if we stayed on the corner as we climbed.

Before I began my ascent up the 203 courses of the ancient and mysterious monument, I looked up to the heavens above the apex. I realized that whoever built this—whenever they built it, wherever they came from, and wherever they had gone—had a definite purpose transcending time and space. After all, the massive monolithic structure had magnetically attracted me since I was a child, and from halfway across the world! I recalled that Plato, Pythagoras, and other great ones had visited the mysteries in the King's Chamber within this secret edifice.

I climbed the first block with some difficulty. It was huge— between four and a half and five feet tall. I helped Pamela, the climber behind me, up the first few blocks by pulling her up. At each block I would push up using my pectoral and arm strength and swing my leg up onto the plateau. This allowed me to simultaneously pull and push myself onto the plateau, landing on my knees. Then I moved into the squatting position and up onto the next block, repeating the process.

Some of the blocks were very high, others were smaller. They seemed to get easier, then harder, then easier. As I climbed I focused on one block at a time, realizing this process was a metaphor for action steps in our lives.

When I was not very far up, a motorcycle drove by in front of the pyramid side we were climbing, and a guard began shining a searchlight on the pyramid. We lay down where we were on the blocks, with as much of our bodies hidden in the shadows as possible. I could feel the cool limestone against me as I lay flat and motionless and the searchlight made its way across the face of the pyramid. After the guard passed, we immediately resumed our ascent.

Pamela was asking for me to wait. As I looked down the southwestern edge of the pyramid to the ground, I was startled to discover how far we had climbed. I felt myself suddenly imagining how easy it would be to tumble down the courses of limestone. I immediately cancelled the fear by focusing on where I was heading. Satisfied that Pamela was close enough to feel comfortable knowing a companion was nearby, I began my ascent again until I came upon another climber, Eric, who had also hurt his ankle on the trip to the pyramid.

Pamela was calling for me to wait for her. Just then the guard on the motorcycle came down the road again with his searchlight shining. We instantly lay down again where we were, hiding in the shadows until he passed. After the guard left, Eric climbed ahead and I waited for Pamela. She breathlessly told me that the searchlight had passed over her prone body. Fortunately, she had concealed herself well.

I continued to climb until I reached Eric again; then I waited for Pamela to get close enough to know I was nearby. We kept this cycle up for the rest of the ascent. As I continued to climb I began to ponder the tremendous degree of precision, skill, and effort that went into laying each of the blocks of the Great Pyramid. I was experiencing just *climbing* it as quite a feat. I could only begin to imagine the purposefully inspired action steps that summated to manifest this six-million-ton mountain made from 2.3 million granite and limestone blocks. Each of these blocks weighed at least 2.5 tons, and many of them weighed 15 tons or more!

After climbing for some time I looked toward the top. It seemed elusive. I kept focusing on the block at hand. I was certain I would make it to the top if I just kept moving up the courses one block at a time. Suddenly I found myself at the summit of the most extraordinary imperial view on earth.

I have visited twenty-one ancient sites of the Mayans, Aztecs, and Olmecs in Mexico, and twenty ancient sites of the Incas and pre-Incas in Peru and Bolivia. Monte Alban was majestic and mysterious in the Mexican mountains. The climb up Huana Picchu at Machu Pichu with my son Michael in the Peruvian Andes, and the view at its peak, was breathtakingly beautiful and inspiring to experience. However, none of these places had the degree of "presence" of this site. I wished that my son could be with me for this experience.

I noticed that at the exact center of the plateau someone had erected a wooden, triangular structure with a thick pole, about 31 feet long, marking the original height of the Great Pyramid at 481.3949 feet. I looked up to the magnificent veil of stars. The crescent moon shone down to our southeast side.

While we sat facing south at the top of the ancient structure, I began to look back on the climb and ponder in detail the significance and meaning of this enigmatic mystery that had stood the test of time. I could easily see that the creator of the Great Pyramid had certainly had a purpose that extended far beyond his or her lifetime. Far above and beyond the megalomania of a king who supposedly built it from the ground up for his tomb in 2500 B.C.!

The creator of the Great Pyramid must have been a highly civilized great thinker, initiated in the sciences of astronomy, mathematics, geometry, engineering, architecture, philosophy, psychology, and symbolism. They must have understood the significance and meaning of symmetry, proportion, and order.

And they must have understood the dimensions of this planet in a way that was not generally understood until the 17th century.

The pyramid's circumference-to-height is the same as the north pole to the equator (1:43,200). The pyramid provides an effective system for translating spherical areas into flat ones. The area of each of its faces is equal to the square of its height. The Great Pyramid was built perfectly east to west and north to south. With dimensions of 755 feet per side, there are less than five inches of variation between the four sides, or less than 0.015 percent variation. This is much more precise than today's buildings.

A bird's-eye view of the three pyramids and the Nile are aligned such that a person viewing the night sky over the same latitude and longitude as the pyramids in 10,500 B.C. observed the Milky Way (Nile) and the belt of Orion (three pyramids). The King's Chamber ventilation shaft is of incredible detail and aligned to the star Orion and constellation Osiris in the night sky in 10,500 B.C. The Queen's Chamber ventilation shaft is aligned to the star Sirius and the constellation Isis in the night sky in 10,500 B.C. The pyramid was designed to incorporate not only pi proportion, but the golden section—phi or 1.6181818 to infinity. Things that make you go hmmmmm!

The creator of the Great Pyramid must have had an imaginative, unified vision far beyond the nearsightedness of mass consciousness that surely existed even in those days. Undoubtedly, he or she knew why they were here. This person certainly had a mission, and must have affirmed it with great enthusiasm and zeal, speaking their words of power about their one purposeful, immortal effect, with the magnetically attractive and creative power of unconditional love for their creation, while realizing and accepting with gratitude both the pain and pleasure on their path of loving purpose.

Wherever she or he came from, they must have known the benefits of planning in great detail, by drawing and writing down both their loves for the monument and their supposed loves and hates or infatuations and resentments. Through writing in time and space, they must have realized that what they truly loved would stand the test of time, and what they had thought they loved or hated would dissolve into an energizing, enlightening, and freeing energy to build what they truly loved.

This person must have known with certainty who they were, and loved themselves as they were. He or she knew where they came from, why they were there, and where they were going, all with gratitude to their Power on High. This must have inspired them to action. And they must have understood the wisdom of fractalizing their immortal purpose into action steps.

The creator of the Great Pyramid was clearly a master organizer and delegator of purposeful directives to many subordinates. Imagine the attention to detail this person must have possessed! Can you imagine the many things that went wrong? For instance, do you suppose that at least a few of those blocks (weighing 5,000 pounds or more) were accidentally dropped from, say, two or three hundred feet?

This person must have organized their one true self and tamed their many subordinate personas. They must have known, deep within, the secrets of magnetically imparting energy into action by focusing on purpose and forsaking distractions. They must have known the secret of controlling one's breath to imbibe energy. They must have known the secret of eating light to stay energized. They must have known the secret of loving the matter at hand and fashioning it into form through energized action. They must have been a divinely inspired being, filled with gratitude for what is, *as it is,* as the secret to getting more of what they loved to be, do, and have.

Wherever this person may have gone after building the Great Pyramid, they left a magical legacy within the mysteries of this amazing structure. There is magic in the questions it forces you to ask. The answers to those questions lead you to other questions, and those answers lead you to generations of more questions and answers. Ultimately, the questions lead back to:

✦ Where did I come from?

✦ Why am I here now?

✦ Where am I going?

✦ Who am I?

The hidden mysteries of the Great Pyramid, by the questions it silently invites, eventually initiate us into the higher-ordered significance and meaning of our lives.

✣ ✣ ✣

I suddenly became aware of a chill from the wind blowing across the pyramid. John, Pamela, and I began our descent. I noticed that we did not have to exert as much energy as we had on the way up. A new set of pains and pleasures were encountered. We could move faster. However, in order to do so, we had to drop down to the plateau of the block below. Sometimes this was more than a little punishing on the knees.

I carefully held back from going too fast. I remembered being very sore after going down the steps at Huana Picchu in a sprint. About halfway down the southwest corner of the pyramid's face we were met by the elderly man in a turban. He told us to wait on a ledge in the shadows until he came for us.

Hiding in the shadows halfway up the southwestern face of the pyramid, we could see the second pyramid standing out in the night. My knees were sore from climbing up onto the blocks. I noticed what I believed were mosquitos attempting to land on my exposed skin. I swatted them away. These mild unpleasantries were worth the peak experience I was having. I knew that I would look back on this night with fondness for the rest of my life.

After a while some of the climbers in the group behind us reached our level. They asked how far it was to the top and what it was like. I told them they were about halfway, and that words could not accurately express what it was like; however, they would know soon enough.

After some time the man in the turban came for us and we climbed down. We were met at the bottom by a guard with an automatic rifle strapped onto him. Fortunately, he had a smile and a very kind face. We walked away from the pyramid and behind some walls of ruins close to the pyramid and were met by our guide. The guard wanted a tip of twenty dollars. John paid the toll. Suddenly we heard loud, angry shouts in Arabic from behind the wall at the southwestern corner of the pyramid. We took off running and hid behind some walls and rocks at the edge of the ruins. In a few minutes our guide came and led us back to the ruins, where we waited for the rest of our group to return.

After our group was reunited we made our way back over the sand dunes, through the graveyard, and across the sand lot to the place we had parked our minivan. We returned to the hotel about 3:30 a.m. Simultaneously exhausted and energized, I showered and lay down for about an hour's sleep before we began a new day of action with energy.

Lao Tsu said, "A tree as big around as you can reach starts with a small seed. A thousand-mile journey starts with one small step." He also said, "When you stretch out a net where birds are going to fly by, what catches a bird is just one eye of the net; but if you make a net with just one eye you will never catch a bird."

Goethe said "Whatever you can do, or dream you can . . . begin it. Boldness has genius, power, and magic in it."

Success in manifesting what you truly love does not happen by accident. It is a consequence of concerted action steps. Each action step is like a single musician that creates part of the symphony of your life. Alone, a single player is not that much to hear. Yet the group—with precise symmetry, proportion, and order—creates something grand, something of infinitely greater magnitude and quality than the sum of its parts. If one player is not in unison, is not focused on the purpose of the orchestra, they throw off the symmetry, proportion, and order of some of the other players. This, in turn, throws off *other* players.

Distractive or reactive action steps—those which are not on purpose—bring about what we cyclically infatuate and resent. They keep our attention sidetracked from what we love to be, do, and have. The synaptic motor units that fail to fire in proper sequence will disorganize and fragment, bringing about excesses and deficiencies of what we love, and cause us to miss the mark.

Concerted action steps—those which are on purpose—bring about what we love. The synaptic motor units that fire their action potentials will wire together in associated pathways by myelinating to bring us about to take action on what we love. You can create a vertically inspired myelinating pathway between your Power on High, power within, and power below as you take action steps now.

Perhaps you have allowed yourself to fall into a rut of being, doing, and having what you have *got* to be, do, and have—instead of clearing a way for what you *love* to be, do, and have. Suppose you were to accept full responsibility for your thoughts (sensory) and actions (motor) as you instantaneously perceive the mysterious beauty in who you are, what you do, and what you have. Imagine what it would feel like to suddenly find yourself pondering the symmetry, proportion, and order of who you are, what you do, and what you have.

Imagine what would happen if you decided to *love* who you are and what you have, and take loving action with attention to detail on what you formerly *had* to do. How surprised would you be to naturally forget what you had to do as you felt the exhilaration of suddenly sliding into the groove, and shooting the vertical tube, in the upward wave of what you love to do now? You may not want to forget about what you have to do. But if you were to look at it in a different light and feel as if you love to do it now, because it aligns with your purpose, can you imagine how it would accelerate your evolution toward your purpose?

Have you ever considered that the quality of your life is directly proportionate to the quality of your questions? How surprised would you be to discover that within you are the answers to your questions? Suppose, upon arising, you were to make your dominant question:

*What is the number one highest priority action step (cause) that will reap the most effect toward my purpose? Can I do it **immediately . . . now . . . today?***

If the answer is yes, do it now! If the answer is no, the next question you can allow yourself to ask is:

Is there one or more primary preliminary action step(s) that will cause the most effect to bring about the highest priority action step?

If so, write it or them down now.

_____

_____

_____

The next question you can begin to ask is:

Can I take action on this today?

If the answer is no then you can continue to further define and write your secondary preliminary action step(s) that will have the most effect on bringing about the primary preliminary action step, which will in turn bring about the highest priority action steps, which will in turn bring about your purposeful goal. Write it or them down now.

_____

_____

_____

If, however, the answer is yes, *take action,* working up the chain of priorities of action steps now. Align and link your goals with your purpose. Break your goal down into as many smaller subgoals or action steps as is necessary to dissolve the fear that roadblocks your purposeful goal.

If you cannot take an action step in confidence now, make an intentional crawl toward your purposeful goal. If you cannot crawl toward your purpose now, because you are lying face down on the horizontal plane like a newborn babe, lift up your head and eyes toward your vision while you worm your way with faith toward it today. Whatever effort you perform builds upon the efforts before, until you find yourself standing upright and walking powerfully and quickly toward your purposeful goal. Place a check mark next to each associated action step as it is completed.

Imagine what would happen if you were to immediately practice perfectly the procedure just described, to the degree that you mysteriously become aware of yourself naturally awakening each day to a greater and greater knowing, with higher and higher certainty, and with firmer and firmer resolute will, as you discover with present-now consciousness an automatic pilot directing you to instantaneous action on your purpose now.

⚜ ⚜ ⚜

Imagine yourself in the middle of a beautiful blue sea. On this sea there are three boats. Boat A is, in fact, a ship. It is a huge, powerful, and extremely swift flagship. Upon its hull is inscribed "Power on High." Admiral Soul is captain of this incredible ship. He has a complement of 144 tried and true crew members he has personally chosen. A golden line extends from the stern of the *Power on High* to the stern of boat B.

Boat B is somewhat smaller and yet quite fast, although not as fast as the *Power on High*. Upon its hull is inscribed "Power Within." The captain of this ship is Commodore White Light of the Soul. He has seven subordinates: Captain Violet, Commander Indigo, Lieutenant Commander Blue, Lieutenant Green, Lieutenant Junior Grade Yellow, Ensign Orange, and Ensign Red. Captain Violet has 3 direct subordinates. Commander Indigo has 5 direct subordinates. Lieutenant Commander Blue has 7 direct subordinates. Lieutenant Green has 9 direct subordinates.

Lieutenant Junior Grade Yellow has 12 direct subordinates. Ensign Orange has 33 direct subordinates. Ensign Red has 49 direct subordinates. A silver line trails from the stern of the *Power Within* to the stern of boat C.

Boat C is somewhat denser and slower than the *Power Within.* Upon its hull is inscribed "Power Below." The captain of this boat is Chief Petty Officer Animal. He has five subordinates: Petty Officer Sight, Petty Officer Hearing, Petty Officer Sensation, Seaman Taste, and Seaman Smell. Seamen Taste and Smell have an affinity for certain brews of spirits that go by the names of Exaggeration, Minimization, Infatuation, and Resentment.

As the *Power on High* moves through the water it leaves behind a wake. From the apex, the wake spreads out and down like a cone. The *Power Within* moves quite well at the center of the wake. If it moves off the center in a tangential direction, it experiences turbulence from the waves it encounters.

When Commodore White Light of the Soul maintains discipline with his seven subordinates (action steps), and they in turn maintain discipline with their subordinates, the ship maintains its true course. When Commodore White Light of the Soul fails to consciously prioritize, and to order his seven subordinates to also prioritize and perform their respective action steps with certainty, there is disorder and chaos. If the seven subordinates are not occupied with their purposeful, prioritized action steps, they tend to be influenced toward distraction by the omission and commission of Chief Petty Officer Animal, who is influenced by his five subordinates, who are in turn influenced by the spirits of Exaggeration, Minimization, Infatuation, and Resentment.

If Commodore Light of the Soul fails to wisely execute his orders to Chief Petty Officer Animal, the Chief will omit and commit away from the perfectly centered and purposeful path and the vessel will experience turbulence. If the Commodore moderates the omissions and commissions, the *Power Below* can be saved from the stormy experience. If the Commodore of the *Power Within* has a will that is too weak and the Chief of the *Power Below* is too set in his ways of omitting and committing, the vessel will be lost.

The *Power Within* may be pulled from side to side like a pendulum by the denser *Power Below* until it finally must follow the golden line to the stern of the *Power on High* and release the silver line to the stern of the disintegrating vessel. The *Power Below* is lost at sea. The *Power on High* and the *Power Within* proceed up the waters to lead a worthy vessel.

No distractive thoughts and no tangential actions, however small, are ever without cost, for the consequences will eventually return. Universal law is not mocked. We will reap the effect of our sowing (cause).

If the seven subordinates are taking action with energy on their purpose, they will tend to influence Chief Petty Officer Animal toward purposeful action with a unified perception of higher order above to within, and govern what the Chief perceives from above and beyond the ordinary senses. Chief Animal will love what he perceives from above to within and act to govern what he perceives from outside to inside with his unified sense above senses. Petty Officers Sight, Hearing, and Sensation, and Seamen Taste and Smell will align and link their functions with Chief Animal. Chief Animal will align his sense above senses to the *Power Within* as he listens to Commodore White Light of the Soul via his inspired seven subordinates and their respective subordinates. Commodore White Light of the Soul freely wills to listen and act on the message of Admiral Soul from within the *Power on High* and the three boats move across the water in a precisely unified and orderly manner with least resistance.

Admiral Soul leads. Commodore White Light of the Soul observes, listens, and acts of his own free will with purposeful, symmetrical action steps to influence Chief Animal to voluntarily follow in accordance with the chain of command. No purposeful thought and no purposeful action, however small, is ever lost, for your consequential reward will finally return. Realize, universal law is not mocked. You will reap the effect of the action steps you sow (cause) today.

A man or woman of greatness, quality, and character with outstanding significance, influence, and power, will sublimate their actions with conviction for a grand purpose with great meaning and significance based on a great principle—a great philosophy—that is expressed clearly through the language of their ordered actions in life.

Joshua 1:8 reads, "Obey everything written in it [universal law]; then you will be prosperous." I invite you to realize that universal law favors no particular person except the one who favors universal law. If you would have universal law favor you, you must align with it and act according to its truth and justice with all your heart and all your soul within you now.

Many stumble over their own opinions and do violence to themselves as they horizontally omit and commit. In so doing, they hit their head against the wall of destiny to become its prisoner. I encourage you to be one of the wise few who walk upright and forward on the vertical narrow path with purposeful thought and inspiring vision, affirming until you can truly feel it with the Power of Love; planning, adjusting, and acting with energy to find yourself mastering your destiny now. Your life is a heroic life, meant to be enjoyed as you act on your purpose while accepting both the pain and the pleasure on the path of your soul's mission. I encourage you to begin to translate, vibrate, and rotate your intangibly formless inspiring purpose, thought, vision, word, and feeling into tangibly manifested form as you take concerted action with energy now.

To liberate more energy,
arrange more order in
your thoughts and actions
on purpose.

ENERGY

Have you ever considered that the highest energy reflects the highest order?

+ The more ordered the arrangement of actions, the more energy is liberated.

+ The less ordered the arrangement of actions, the more energy is imprisoned.

+ Higher order equals higher energy.

+ Higher energy equals higher acceleration multiplied by what we call time equals velocity, and therefore higher frequency.

+ Higher velocity and frequency of action in what we call time multiplied by a greater quantity of what we call matter equals greater force.

+ Greater force multiplied by a greater distance in what we call space equals greater work.

+ Greater work in less time, affecting greater levels of space and time, is intensity.

+ Great intensity equals great power.

Energy cannot be created or destroyed; it can only be transformed. To liberate more energy, arrange more order in your thoughts and actions on purpose. Prioritize your action steps with meaning. Can you imagine the incredible amount of energy you would liberate if you were to act on the 5% of action steps that give you 50% of your results toward fulfilling your purpose? Have you ever asked yourself, What are the 20% of my actions that bring me 80% of my results?

In Isaac Asimov's *Understanding Physics,* Sir Isaac Newton's third law of motion reveals, "Whenever one body exerts a force on a second body, the second body exerts a force on the first body. These forces are equal in magnitude and opposite in direction." Any matter on which you exert any force exerts an equal force on you. If you are exerting force on a purposeful goal, a purposeful goal is exerting force on you. What you are taking action on is taking action on you. Truly, what you are seeking is seeking you, *so direct your energetic force toward what you love.*

Life begins with a first breath and ends with a last breath. Air contains the electricity that charges our vital capacitor with energy. Breathing, posture, physiology, and function are inter-related in expressing our vital potential energy. Energy is infinite and is universally available to the one with greater order. Higher-ordered breathing transforms and liberates energy. Disordered breathing stifles and imprisons energy.

Breathing only from the chest is short, shallow, disordered breathing that depends upon several muscles of the neck to elevate the rib cage. It is the 80% effort that returns 20% results. It can literally be a pain in the neck because the muscles manifest tension due to the stressful breathing. Symmetrical, diaphragmatic breathing, which will be described shortly, is the 20% effort that returns 80% results.

Greater inhalations than exhalations excite. Greater exhalations than inhalations sedate. Balance inhalations with exhalations. Balance long slow breaths with short fast breaths. Both are useful.

Balanced, even, symmetrical breathing generates great energy and brings the power within and the power below into synergistic present-now consciousness with the Power on High. Uneven, unbalanced, asymmetrical breathing brings the higher-minded power within and the lower-minded power below into a consciousness of guilt about the past or fear of the future.

The higher-minded power within directs our striated skeletal muscles. The lower-minded power below directs our smooth, involuntary muscles. If you are in future fear and past guilt, the lower-minded power below rules the higher-minded power within you and you omit what is purposeful and commit what is perpendicular or tangential to what is purposeful. Balanced, diaphragmatic breathing keeps you on purpose.

Have you ever noticed how a baby breathes? Babies "belly breathe" by innately utilizing their diaphragm. They continue their diaphragmatic breathing until they are about 12 years of age. Perhaps it contributes to their boundless energy. The diaphragm is the heart of the lymphatic system. Symmetrical, diaphragmatic breathing cycles pump the lymphocytes and fatty plasma through the lymphatic system, and surround and block off foreign invaders such as bacteria.

Symmetrical breathing cycles, which begin and end with the diaphragm, balance and bring order between the sympathetic and parasympathetic nervous system. Symmetrical diaphragmatic breathing balances acid and alkaline pH. Symmetrical diaphragmatic breathing stimulates both the left and right cerebral hemispheres and activates the corpus callosum, the highest evolved, higher-minded part of the brain.

You can easily learn diaphragmatic breathing as you practice perfect breathing a little each day.

+ Begin by standing erect or lying supine. Place your hands upon your abdomen.

+ As you inhale through your nose for a slow count of seven, let your abdomen protrude. Feel it move with your hands.

+ Hold your air for a slow count of seven.

+ As you exhale through your nose for a slow count of seven, use your hands to feel your abdomen pull in.

+ Continue pulling your abdomen in and tighten it for a slow count of seven.

+ Repeat this cycle for a total of seven cycles.

Practice this exercise perfectly for one week and begin to add cycles until you can complete 12 perfect cycles. Keep practicing for 21 consecutive days. After 21 days of practice, you will have mastered diaphragmatic breathing to the point that you can easily experiment with both slow and fast cycles of breathing.

Practice diaphragmatic breathing for periods of five, ten, fifteen minutes, or more. If you feel like you are going to fall backwards, put your back against a wall. Notice the feeling you experience as you complete the exercise. Realize that as you control your breathing, you control your mental magnetic power to take action with energy now.

Water is the basic constituent of all living things. It is the source from which nature comes and nature goes. Scientists estimate that our bodies are composed of between 70 and 90% water. Our cells, tissues, organs, vital fluids, and secretions are largely water.

Water is our most precious nutrient and oldest remedy. It promotes regularity, replenishes lost fluids, and dilutes the minerals that pass through the kidneys, helping to prevent kidney stones. Water bathes our cells, tissues, and organs, and cleans and rejuvenates us in a number of ways, within and without. Water is better than low-calorie: it has *no* calories! If you were to drink two 8-ounce glasses upon arising you would be giving your power below a great gift. Properly watered, it can more purposefully serve you. Drinking seven 8-ounce glasses a day is wise.

Developing rhythms in sleeping, eating, and eliminating brings greater order. Eating before the sun goes down and rising before the sun comes up allows the power within and the power below to align with the circadian rhythms of the sun. When our neuroendocrine systems are aligned with the circadian rhythms of the sun there is greater order, and therefore abundance of energy liberated purposefully. Benjamin Franklin spoke wisely when he said, "Early to bed, early to rise makes a man healthy, wealthy, and wise."

If we are arrhythmic in our cycles we align our neuroendocrine systems with the ultradian rhythms of the moon. How surprised would you be to discover that in ancient times the sun was revered for its dependability and rhythm, while the moon was considered to be flighty and erratic in its cycles? No wonder that someone who is extremely emotional, erratic, and impulsive to the point of irresponsible conduct is called a "luna-tic."

Have you ever eaten a fat-laden meal and discovered that you suddenly felt groggy and sleepy? You can easily understand that a greasy or fat-laden meal taxes the smooth muscles of the digestive system controlled by the lower-minded power below, causing it to draw energy from the higher-minded power within that controls the striated skeletal muscles which take action on your purpose.

I invite you to consider that the highest energy-generating foods are those that seek the sun. Greens and other colored vegetables, whole grains, legumes, fruits, nuts, flesh, fish, eggs, and dairy all have their place. A wise intake ratio is approximately 20% greens, 20% grains, 20% legumes, 20% fruit, and the other 20% a combination of nuts, fish, flesh, eggs, or dairy.

+ Life-generating foods—such as soaked and germinated seeds, nuts, grains, and legumes—are highly life-sustaining and energy-generating.

+ Fresh, unprocessed raw fruits and vegetables are life- and energy-sustaining.

+ Foods that are cooked are life-decaying yet energy-sustaining.

+ Any raw or cooked food that is not fresh is life-decaying and energy-draining.

+ Foods with additives, or those that have been processed, refined, or preserved are bioacidic and life- and energy-decaying.

For optimum energy, eat a balance of fresh raw and fresh cooked foods. Eat foods that rot, but eat them while they are fresh. Raw foods stimulate red blood cell production. Cooked foods stimulate white blood cell production. Both are necessary and balance the other for optimum energy. Remember, eat to live for your purpose; do not live for the pleasure or pain of eating.

Prioritized actions, ordered breathing, and abundant pure water form a tripod that stands you up on the vertical plane toward your purpose. If you were to add regular body rhythms and balanced, moderate food intake, you would have five spokes on a wheel, making you so well rounded you could immediately move toward your purpose with incredible energy now.

Prioritize your actions to your core purpose and align your physical habits to support it. You can easily find yourself breathing diaphragmatically and drinking plenty of water. Suppose that following your purpose required you to lose some sleep or travel extensively, breaking your daily rhythm. Or perhaps you find yourself in circumstances that do not allow for the best or wisest food intake. Improvise and adapt to whatever is available to you at the present time. All things in moderation, including moderation. If you were to be obsessive about something, be obsessive about writing, reading, listening to and saying your words of power, and asking yourself what action you are taking with energy immediately to accomplish your purpose.

I encourage you to prioritize and link your goals and action steps to your purpose today. You, the power within, and your lower-minded power below have a divinely inspired mission. The power within that is you is immortal. As you can clearly see, you—the higher-minded power within—are connected to the Power on High. The Power on High is the ocean and you—the power within—are the wave. As you begin to become aware that you—the higher-minded power within—are infinitely connected to the Power on High, and that the Power on High is beyond time and space, I invite you to realize that the lower-minded power below is mortal and exists in time and space.

Your mission, if you choose to accept it, is to follow the pole star of purpose in time and space as you live your earthly life. In a sense, you only have so much time and energy, so prioritize your goals and action steps to your purpose. Do what is most on purpose, delegate what is necessary to support your purpose if you can, and forsake what is left with love. Nothing can give your life more meaning than your purpose, so waste no energy on tangents and if you do, realize that maximum evolution toward your purpose occurs at the transition from lower order to higher order. Even in your chaotic entropic mistakes there is a divinely blessed system seeking syntropic higher order, guiding you toward a conservation of energy toward your purpose from:

+ Unconsciously unconscious to
+ Semiconsciously unconscious to
+ Semiconsciously semiconscious to
+ Consciously semiconscious to
+ Consciously conscious to
+ Superconsciously conscious to
+ Superconsciously superconscious.

You have a choice. You may not want to accelerate your evolution of consciousness toward your vision, inspiration, and purpose now. But if you did choose to do so, you can easily see the incredible higher-ordered energy and power you would generate toward your purposeful goal.

Imagine what it would feel like if you were to liberate higher and higher orders of energy, empowering you to take prioritized action steps on your purposeful goals today. Imagine what would happen if you were to take immediate action while you continue to feel the incredibly empowering feeling that energizes you from above, down, inside, and outside of you as you magnetically move toward and attract the perfect people, ideas, and circumstances to fulfill your purposeful goals now. I encourage you to take purposeful action with energy on the matter at hand today.

As we resonate in phase with higher-ordered matter, we open ourselves to attract, move toward, and electro-magnetically phase lock with the perfect people, places, things, and events (matter) that are the next level for us to learn to unconditionally love and appreciate.

MATTER

The syllable "ma" in the word "matter" is universal for mother in many of the world's languages as far back as Sanskrit. The word "mater" is from Old English, derived from the Germanic "moder." The word "materies" is Latin for tree trunk or source of growth. Matter is like a tangible, formful mother of manifestation, and energy is like an intangible, formless father of manifestation.

You can easily see that a coin cannot exist without two sides, a head and a tail. The coin of manifestation cannot take its place in time without energy and matter. As you begin to understand that the head and tail of a coin are opposite yet complementary sides that make up a coin, I invite you to realize that both energy and matter are complementary forces that support one another to conceive and birth manifestation. Matter without energy is lifeless, and energy without matter is expressionless.

Matter is a series of patterns of energy materializing in particles of relative disordered monopolistic entropy. Energy is matter evolving toward relatively fewer and relatively ordered patterns of dematerializing matter in waves of relative, ordered, dipolistic syntropy.

Matter tangibly occupies space and can be perceived by one or more of our senses. Energy is the capacity of physical systems of matter to move in the direction of its force. Matter is the cause of energy (effect) and energy is the cause of matter (effect). Therefore, cause equals effect and effect equals cause infinitely. We can perceive the effects of energy with our five senses, but we cannot perceive energy itself, although we might perceive energy's cause (matter).

Matter is the tangible form of stuff we take energetic action on to manifest our purposefully focused vision. Realize that the matter at hand is subtly affected by our resonate energy (electromagnetic charge) and that matter has its own resonant energy. We and the world we experience are like parts of a great chemistry equation on a grand scale, evolving us from ionic bonding toward more noble covalent bonding. We evolve from the tangential ionic charge of opposite situational values exchanged by our emotional infatuation and resentment cycles toward covalent matter that is congruent with our purposeful values. If we cannot feel love and gratitude for the matter around us, we are locked in resonating phase with the wavefront of what we infatuate or resent, and we are destined to repeat it until we finally learn to love both the perceived goods and perceived bads of the matter at hand.

Whatever our thoughts are focused on is what we attract and move toward. If our thoughts are directed by our emotionally charged judgments of infatuation and resentment of the matter at hand, then we repeatedly find ourselves repeating the matter at hand—perhaps in a new form, yet with the same essence of energy as the matter at hand which we exaggerated or minimized, and in which we failed to find the symmetry, proportion, and order.

In order to solve a paradox, we must rise above it into integrative unity and choose not to take the side of good or evil, pain or pleasure, positive or negative, exaggeration or minimization, infatuation or resentment. If we allow our perceptions to fall into one side or the other, we become a part of the paradox until we decide to stop and realize the fear of the future in guilt about the past, and the guilt about the past in fear of the future, the evil in good and good in evil, the pain in pleasure and pleasure in pain, the negative in positive and positive in negative, the minimization in exaggeration and exaggeration in minimization, the resentment in infatuation and infatuation in resentment, the science in religion and the religion in science.

Whatever matter you encounter, in whatever station in life you find yourself, and wherever you find yourself, convince yourself to love the matter at hand. I invite you to realize that until you truly love the matter at hand, you will continue to experience it. The form of the matter may change, but the essence of it will remain the same until you infinitely transcend the matter with loving action and presence. You cannot skip over this evolutionary step of consciousness relating to the matter at hand. The next level of matter and the next level of resonating consciousness relating to the next level of relatively nobler matter at hand is dependent on who you are today, what you think today, what you feel today, and what you do or refrain from doing now.

You have a choice. You can remain paralyzed or destructively active by fear and guilt, or you can purposefully focus your presence now on the matter at hand. You may not desire to be present now with the matter at hand, but if you were to find yourself beginning to realize that all life is designed to seek relatively higher order and symmetry, and that the greater the order and symmetry we perceive in the matter at hand in greater degrees of time and space, the greater the consciousness we resonantly express and tune to and the greater the energy and higher refined matter we attract and move toward, you would naturally understand and agree that experiencing loving presence now with the matter at hand is clearly essential to manifest what you love.

There are many who consider transient, tangential matters as "shortcuts." These people are sleeping. They do not perceive their side trips as tangential. They are focused horizontally, avoiding pain and pursuing pleasure—only to be disillusioned as they discover pain on the opposite side of pleasure, and reluctant to find pleasure on the opposite side of pain. Having missed the point of purpose they find their life pointless and painful, motivated by future fear and past guilt as they neglect the matter at hand.

The few truly wise realize that the only true shortcut is to link and align each action on the matter at hand with their purpose even if it seems far removed. The truly wise realize that the only shortcut is on the vertical, narrow path of purpose at the golden mean of past and future, pain and pleasure, good and evil, positive and negative, infatuation and resentment.

The truly wise focus on the orderly details of the matter at hand (means) and adjust and fine tune their actions accordingly to bring about their purposeful ends. The greater the detailed order we perceive in the matter at hand, the greater the consciousness we resonate with to bring about the matter we love. To be present with the matter you love, act with loving presence now on the details of the matter at hand.

Focusing with ever finer detail, through our five senses, on the matter at hand takes our consciousness out of fear of the future and guilt about the past and brings us into loving presence now with the matter at hand. Focusing on ever finer motor expressions directed on or at the matter at hand leads our consciousness into an awakened state of presence now with the matter at hand. Writing about the matter at hand involves the memory and imagination of the five senses. If we balance the perceived positives and negatives of the matter at hand to a point of symmetry, proportion, and order by the fine motor skill of writing, we unite our sensory and motor systems on the truth of the matter at hand and increase our sense of presence with the matter.

The more presence we experience, the more illusive ions (illusions) we dissolve that separate past and future, fear and guilt, infatuation and resentment, positive and negative, good and evil, pleasure and pain, and the more we easily comprehend the true worth, blessing, lesson, and beauty of the matter at hand. As we comprehend the true worth, blessing, lesson, and beauty of the matter at hand, we naturally find ourselves experiencing gratitude for what is the matter at hand, as it is, tuning us to resonate in phase with higher-ordered matter.

As we resonate in phase with higher-ordered matter, we open ourselves to attract, move toward, and electromagnetically phase lock with the perfect people, places, things, and events (matter) that are the next level for us to learn to unconditionally love and appreciate. Having risen above the perceived paradox of the matter behind us, we find ourselves discovering a new perceived paradox of exaggeration and minimization, infatuation and resentment, to rise above in our perceptions with unified love. For each level of matter we take action with energy on, we experience equal ratios of pain and pleasure, as we dissolve infatuations and resentments, goods and evils, exaggerations and minimizations, positives and negatives, fear of the future and guilts about the past. The more details that we experience, with gratitude and love, about the matter at hand, the more freedom we have to experience the matter we love.

Suppose you were to focus your thought on your inspired vision and calling as you affirm your words of power, feeling the unconditional love for your purposeful vision and having the disciplined courage to write your action plan down in time and space as you take action with energy on matter with attention to infinite detail, and experience present-time consciousness now with greater levels of higher-ordered matter and increased energy and greater power. Imagine what would happen if you were to suddenly take action with incredible energy immediately on the matter at hand. How surprised would you be to find yourself truly being, achieving, and obtaining what and who you love to be, do, and have? Imagine what it would feel like if you were to experience present-time consciousness with the matter available while taking energetic action. How surprised would you be to suddenly realize that the more present-time consciousness you experience with the available matter, the more you find yourself discovering higher quality matter is made available? You can easily picture that the more patiently present now you are with the matter at hand, the greater the present you will find yourself mysteriously manifesting underneath the fir tree of life.

I encourage you to awaken from the shadows of fear and guilt as you purposefully focus your thoughts in the light of your inspiring vision, affirming it with your words of power as you feel your vision with the power of love and write your loves in fine detail, while taking action with energy and loving presence now on the matter at hand, until you find yourself beholding the spiritual essence of the matter, with gratitude to your Power on High for what was, what is, and what shall be.

Gratitude tunes you to the
inspiring angle of light from
the Power on High.

GRATITUDE

It was a moonless summer night on top of a mountain near Taos, New Mexico. My friend Gene and I were waiting to enter a small Indian tent about four feet high. We were anxious about the unknown as we waited. Crawling into the ceremonial tent on my knees, I entered a very small area with a circular pit in the center. I sat on some animal skins facing the pit. Gene sat next to me.

Twelve of us were seated inside: six women facing six men. Four large, hot rocks — glowing red in the darkness — faced east, west, north, and south. The Native American leading the ceremony gave his invocation as the temperature began to rise.

As I began to feel the heat from the glowing rocks, Gene leaned over and said he was feeling very nauseated. The ceremony leader asked if he wanted to leave. Gene said no. The leader suggested that Gene lie down and stretch out between the rocks and people. Gene did so, and later told me that this allowed him to breathe slightly cooler air.

My lower-minded power below began to react to the discomfort. My brain noise justified and defended, exaggerated and minimized what I would, should, and could do to make the discomfort go away.

I knew that the Native American Indians had used this ceremony as a purification process and as part of an initiation into a spiritual experience, but at the moment I just knew that I felt miserable and my friend was lying face down gasping for air. It suddenly occurred to me that my power below had entrapped itself in a paradox between getting away from the discomfort and avoiding the embarrassment of leaving.

I felt Gene's posterior tibial pulse. It was weak and barely palpable. I asked him if he was all right, and he answered, "Barely." I asked him if he wanted to leave, and he said no.

After what seemed like a long time, the leader opened the tent flap briefly and more glowing rocks were brought in and placed at the center of the pit. Some water was sprinkled on the rocks. The steam seemed to burn my lungs as I inhaled. The Indian threw some herbs on the rocks; this gave off a pleasant aroma.

It seemed to get more hellish. One person excused himself and left, gasping for air. I checked Gene's tibial pulse again. I could not feel it. I asked him if he was all right. He feebly answered, "Yes."

I began to wonder if I should take Gene and get out. It would have been a convenient reason for me to leave. The power within me—my true higher-minded nature—was like a non-judgmental observer watching the lower-minded part of me. Suddenly I remembered that the only way to solve a paradox is to rise above it.

I began to mentally send love and gratitude to the Power on High and the people in my life. I touched Gene and imagined that I was receiving love from the Power on High and sending the healing power of love through me to him. I then silently communicated love to each person in my life. I thanked each of them for how they had impacted my life.

I visualized myself in their presence, experiencing my gratitude and love for them. Suddenly, I realized the discomfort had eased considerably. I spent the rest of the time in the sweatlodge in a state of inspiration. After almost three hours, we emerged truly grateful!

✴ ✴ ✴

Have you ever considered that an attitude of appreciative, conscious awareness, with recognition, acknowledgment, and gratitude to the Power on High and every person, place, idea and event you have received an experience with, determines your altitude (on Abraham Maslow's hierarchy) of being, doing, and having? What you appreciate appreciates you. What you depreciate depreciates you. Gratitude tunes you to the circadian rhythms of poise, and ingratitude tunes you to the ultradian rhythm of relative charge. Gratitude is health-promoting, and ingratitude is health-destroying. Whatever quality, value, significance, and magnitude in the people, places, ideas, events, and matter you have gratitude for raises your value. Truly, gratitude is the beginning of greatness and inestimable worth from self and others.

The 19th century British philosopher Herbert Spencer wrote, "Gratitude is the tune of the angels." Gratitude tunes you to the inspiring angle of light from the Power on High. Gratitude tunes the gut instinct, the intuitive mind, and the open heart to receive the light of inspiration. The greater the magnitude of love and gratitude you experience, the more vertical and direct the angle of light with which you resonate.

Many people pray for this or that, but the omnipotent and omniscient Power from on High that rules the universe knows your heart and every need, want, and desire; and love is already infinitely known. You do not have to convince your Power on High. The Power on High is already delivering in time and space, in electromagnetic resonating phase with your thoughts, feelings, and actions. Convince yourself to the point of certainty with your words of power, and take concerted action with energy, faith, and confidence, and the Power on High supports you. Make gratitude your first and last prayer, and make your life a living prayer of gratitude. Realize that an open heart full of gratitude is the key that unlocks the pearly gate of the Power on High.

Every cloud has a golden sunbeam or brilliant platinum starlight on the other side. I invite you to begin to see the sunbeams and starlight behind the apparent clouds in your life. Look for the blessing in every crack, crevice, and turn in your life. Each crisis has an opportunity around the corner if you will search it out. Whatever your innermost dominant thought and feeling is focused on is what you attract, become, or move toward—so focus on the blessing. What would it feel like if you were to immediately find yourself convinced that the tangible world and the intangible universe are conspiring to manifest your success now? What would happen in your life if you were to suddenly discover you have become an inverse paranoid?

The greater the quantity and quality the moments of gratitude you experience, the greater the quantity and quality of communion you experience with your omniscient, omnipotent Source. The greater the quantity and quality of your communion in present-now consciousness with your Source, the greater the inner genius is made known within you, opening you to the unfolding of your purpose, crystal-clear clarity of thought, intensely colorful and vivid vision, and the inner calling of the parental Voice on High from above, down, and inside you. The loving feeling of knowing within knowing within knowing, and acting on the urge to write it down, leads you to the perfect time, the perfect place, the perfect event, the perfect matter, to take action with incredible energy to manifest who and what you love to be, do, and have.

Suppose you were to begin to find the blessings in every person, place, idea, event, and thing in your life. What would it be like to find yourself discovering, in incredible detail, the symmetry, proportion, and order in each area of your life now? You can begin to clearly see that what is, is perfect as it is, and discover that everything is unfolding perfectly for you in its own way, in its own day, and its own place.

Perhaps you have perceived your early family life as having been dysfunctional. You may have had the illusion that your life is dysfunctional because you perceived that your father or mother was not there for you when you were growing up. You might discover that you have held the illusion that your father, mother, brother, sister, wife, husband, or other person was "always" bad and "never" good, or "always" good and "never" bad. Realize that both are lies. They are perceptual exaggerations or minimizations of what was and what is, and they determine what will be.

Your perceived past determines your future as you create with symmetrical vision, inspiration, and purpose or with asymmetrical desperation, exaggeration, minimization, infatuation, and resentment. Perhaps one or both parents were alcoholics. Perhaps one or more of your parents molested you. Whatever the story is, there is a hidden order behind what you perceive. Sir Isaac Newton stated that every action has an equal and opposite balancing action. Albert Einstein asserted with his theory of relativity that energy and matter are interchangeable waves and particles in an eternal, infinite dance. I invite you to consider that if you are correct in your perceived victimhood, then Newton's Third Law of Motion and the Law of Conservation of Energy and Matter are wrong, and I await your thesis. Chaos is just an illusion that you need to believe until you decide to choose to find the hidden order behind the veil of perception on the path of unconditional love and gratitude.

Ask yourself what payoff you get for holding someone else responsible for your life. Do you get to avoid responding to life's events? Do you get to assign excess positive charge to your opinion of yourself? Do you get to assign deficient positive charge (excess negative charge) to your opinion of other(s)? Do you get to stay comfortable in your primal, paradigmal box sealed by fear and guilt? Do you get to reinforce your perceived level of self-worth by hiding from your guilt about the past and blaming someone else for what turns out to have been perfect after all? What have you done that is so bad?

How surprised would you be to discover the freedom in examining and owning all that has happened in your life, and moving up on your path toward your purpose? How has your painful experience helped you? Every pain has an equal pleasure somewhere—in one or more of the seven areas of life, in one or more points in time. What pleasure did you get that you are not owning now? When? In what area of your life: physical, mental, social, financial, career, family, spiritual? How did this experience help others? When? In what area of their lives: physical, mental, social, financial, career, family, spiritual?

Conversely, every pleasure has an equal pain somewhere—in one or more of the seven areas of life, in one or more points in time. What pain did your perceived perpetrator experience that you are not acknowledging now?

As you look back on your life, what "breakdowns" became the seeds for the biggest breakthroughs in your life? Perhaps a physical breakdown (your own or someone else's) caused your heart to open spiritually and your mind to become stronger, to the degree of having a will of steel. Perhaps it brought your family together in a loving, common purpose. Perhaps it birthed a new career helping others. Perhaps it was the impetus for a greater outreach to help others on a national or planetary scale. Perhaps it benefited you or others financially. Perhaps it taught you or someone else to become physically stronger or healthier.

Perhaps a mental "breakdown" (your own or someone else's) became the seed for mental reorganization that resulted in a higher level of functioning. Perhaps it led you to use your physical gifts to excel. Perhaps it helped you in your career, helping others to become more emotionally integrated. Perhaps it helped you bring your family together. Perhaps it opened your heart spiritually. Perhaps it helped you encounter a new society of people who taught you so much. Perhaps you were financially rewarded.

Suppose you were a social "outcast" as a child. Did it help you to excel in your social contact with others and gain respect? Perhaps it gave you an inner desire to get ahead and make money. Perhaps it made you physically or mentally stronger or healthier. Perhaps it motivated you to excel in your career. Perhaps it guided you toward a closer relationship with your mother, father, husband, wife, grandmother, grandfather, brother, or sister. Perhaps it opened your heart to your one true being, instead of the society of false personas within you.

Suppose you had a financial "disaster." How did it serve your highest good? Did it humble you to the Power on High? Did it make you physically and/or mentally healthier? Did it teach you to appreciate the beauty in all social circles? Did it help you to finally do what you love, and love what you do? Did it help you to break through to greater unity and purpose with your family?

Maybe you "lost" the career you had identified yourself with. What did you gain? Did it help you to finally do what you love and love what you do? Did it give you more time with your family? Did it free you spiritually? Did it put you in the right place at the right time to meet the right people and experience the right events to make the right deal to improve your career, finances, or social status?

Suppose you had a family "breakdown." How did this also lead to a breakthrough? Did a neighbor, aunt, uncle, parent, or sibling begin to fill in the time and space you perceived as lost? Perhaps it guided you to bring families together or benefited you financially. Did it prompt you to begin your spiritual quest to discover that the only true parents are our Parents on High? Did it make you physically and/or mentally stronger because of what you contributed to the family? Did it lead you to a new group of surrogate family members?

Suppose you had a spiritual "crisis." Did it birth the beginning of a phoenix-like rise from the crash and burn to new heights? Did it help you find a new career? Did it plant the seeds for a spiritual breakthrough? Did it make you mentally stronger? Did it help you to seek out new social circles? Did it help you to focus more on finances? Did it guide you to seek your family? Did it guide you to increase your focus on your physical condition?

I encourage you to complete the truth, gratefulness, and unconditional love for events form on pages 150 and 151 now.

As you discover beauty, you uncover love and gratitude. Gratitude opens your heart to receive inspiration. The greater your inspiration, the higher your self-worth and the higher the altitude of being, doing, and having you experience on Maslow's hierarchy.

TRUTH, GRATEFULNESS, AND UNCONDITIONAL LOVE FOR EVENTS FORM

"Judgment Collapse Form"

Column 1 "Good" events (+)	Column 2 Drawbacks to me (–)	Column 3 Drawbacks to others (–)
Great physical shape	Less time for mental and spiritual activities	Intimidates some people
Strong spiritual experience	Sometime I feel misunderstood	Others feel excluded
Learned new information	Must use it or be miserable	Spouse must listen to me talk about it
Great job	Less time for sports	Family misses me when I'm gone
Came into money	Must learn to invest wisely	Some people resent me for having it
Daughter born	Financial challenge; loss of sleep	Loss of time with spouse
President of social club	Less quiet time for self	Less time for family

EXAMPLE

When positives outweigh negatives, you become attracted and infatuated. When negatives outweigh positives, you become repelled and resentful. When positives equal negatives (equal in degree, kind, magnitude, quantity, and quality), they **collapse** into each other, enlightening you to become accepting and loving. To love some person, place, thing, idea, or event is to accept what you like and dislike about it. Communication is maximized in the love state. Whatever you are able to love builds love in you. People, places, things, ideas, and events are reflections of you.

The seven areas of life are:
physical, spiritual, mental, career, financial, family, and social.

Column 4 "Bad" events (–)	Column 5 Benefits to me (+)	Column 6 Benefits to others (+)
Mononucleosis at 17	Got me to stop and look deeply into my life	Helped sister find her purpose in life as a healer
Fundamentalism scared me as child	Taught me foundation of spirituality	Other people need this belief system at times
Embarrassed in public	Taught me to act and dress more appropriately	Others learned from my mistake
Failed important test	Set me off on my lifetime mission	Someone else filled the space
Lost money on bad investment	Made me grow spiritually	Helped me help others with spiritual/financial principles
Parents divorced when I was 12	Neighbor and uncle became fatherly	Mother became independent
Lost my job	I found something I love to do	Someone more suited filled vacuum
	EXAMPLE	

For free copies of this form, call (713) 334-0777 or write to:
Dr. Richard Bellamy, 2400 Augusta Drive, Suite 210, Houston, TX 77057

TRUTH, GRATEFULNESS, AND UNCONDITIONAL LOVE FOR EVENTS FORM

"Judgment Collapse Form"

Column 1 "Good" events (+)	Column 2 Drawbacks to me (−)	Column 3 Drawbacks to others (−)

When positives outweigh negatives, you become attracted and infatuated. When negatives outweigh positives, you become repelled and resentful. When positives equal negatives (equal in degree, kind, magnitude, quantity, and quality), they **collapse** into each other, enlightening you to become accepting and loving. To love some person, place, thing, idea, or event is to accept what you like and dislike about it. Communication is maximized in the love state. Whatever you are able to love builds love in you. People, places, things, ideas, and events are reflections of you.

The seven areas of life are:
physical, spiritual, mental, career, financial, family, and social.

Column 4 "Bad" events (−)	Column 5 Benefits to me (+)	Column 6 Benefits to others (+)

For free copies of this form, call (713) 334-0777 or write to:
Dr. Richard Bellamy, 2400 Augusta Drive, Suite 210, Houston, TX 77057

Now that you have completed the truth, gratefulness, and unconditional love for events form you can easily see the symmetry, proportion, and order throughout your life. You can clearly see that there is inherent beauty in all of the people, places, ideas, events, and things throughout your universe that evolves around you infinitely. The shiver of bliss and inspired tears you immediately experience as you realize the noblest beauty present in your life makes all of your past life infinitely meaningful and worthwhile, in order to experience this moment now. The greatness of your life can be measured by the greatness of gratitude in a single moment. Imagine if your life were a collection of exceptional moments of unconditional love and gratitude.

Suppose you were to stand with your hands at your side, palms open and facing forward. Or you might want to raise your arms above your head with your hands facing up. Notice what it's like as you raise your head and eyes directly upward and close your eyes gently. As you continue to stand upright in inspiration, and begin to appreciate and feel gratitude for the people, places, ideas, events, and things that have truly blessed you in your life and helped you become who you are today, you can continue your thankfulness until you feel your heart open and you experience an incredible state of unconditional love. Tears of inspired bliss come pouring forth as you clearly see how all these people and events played a magnificent role in the divinely designed unfoldment of your life.

As your heart is expanded and opened in its magnetism and your tears are flowing, you can ask your Power on High for its guidance, its wisdom, and its message. Wait for the message from your innermost resource of your power within until it arrives in your consciousness. As you get your vision, voice, or feeling—or any combination of vision, voice, and feeling—

write it down. Experience the message, the messenger, and the giver of the message with love and thankfulness now. Can you imagine the impact this exercise would have on your life if you were to perform it upon arising each morning and before re-tiring each evening, and take action with energy on your vision and calling?

You might decide not to count your blessings in every situation, every way, every day. But if you consider the alternative —a self-imposed inferno of despair—you might find yourself instantaneously becoming aware of the mysteriously beautiful symmetry, proportion, and order everywhere around you today.

Gratitude merges your grand plan with Divine Design into a syntropic partnership of manifestation. I encourage you to find the symmetrical, proportionate, ordered, beatific blessing in each person, event, place, and thing. What would happen in your life if, each time some person, event, or thing pushed your buttons, you were to have the courage to immediately stop and ask yourself:

- ✦ Where have I done that to the same degree in one or more of the seven areas of life?

- ✦ In which area did I do it: physical, mental, spiritual, career, social, relationships, financial?

- ✦ How did it benefit me? How did it benefit others?

- ✦ How was it a drawback to me? How was it a draw-back to others?

- ✦ How did my button-pusher's actions benefit me?

- ✦ How were these actions a drawback to me? How has the drawback been a benefit to me? In which area of my life?

Do you suppose that, if you were to perform this exercise daily, you would experience greater quality and quantity of gratitude in your life?

I encourage you to hold your meaningful purpose, thought, vision, and calling indelibly imprinted on your heart with love; and to write and take energetic action with gratitude on what was, what is, and what will be the matter at hand. Persist with gratitude until, during, and after what you love exists in time and space.

"Be thou wise, and fear not thy tribulations, for out of chaos is brought to birth a star."

– Author unknown

PERSEVERANCE

It has been said, "That which persists exists, and that which exists persists." I invite you to understand that what persists as a formless, principled idea eventually exists as a form in time and space; and that which exists in time and space persists as a conceptual idea whose time has come for manifestation.

Suppose you were to convince yourself to have the courage to persevere in experiencing incredible determination now. Imagine what would happen during and after you persevere relentlessly, to a place where you find yourself manifesting what you love. Imagine what it would feel like to begin manifesting your purposefully inspired vision now.

Persevere in your meaningful purpose, with principled conceptualization, holding your vision continuously before you, with your calling within you, your feeling drawing you, your grand plan before you, your action expressed from you, with energy on your matter at hand, with gratitude for all that was, is, and will be.

Decisiveness and perseverance are the omnipotent power that sustains you until the principles of purpose, plus thought with vision and affirmation, along with feeling and writing, plus action with energy on matter, combined with gratitude, finally delivers your manifestation. Many fall away to chase a transient tangent and find themselves "victims" of their own designs. Do not get so involved with the emotionally charged value of the means that your vision of the end purpose is forgotten. The truly wise persevere, on purpose, realizing that the path of true purpose costs—and pays—greatly.

Persevere, on purpose, toward your love, and enlighten your load of tangents. To maximize what you love, prioritize and prune your tree of transient values (how and what you *have* to be, do, and have; how and what you *ought* to be, do, and have; how and what you *need* to be, do, and have; how and what you *want* to be, do, and have; how and what you *desire* to be, do, and have) so that you have many options to make a choice to be, do, and have, how and what you love.

The inherent wisdom of nature does not throw away old processes. It develops new processes of a higher order, and which are fewer in number than the old processes. Sacrifice your many lower-powered transient values on the altar of the Power on High to make way for your fewer and greater purposeful loves to manifest.

I am not suggesting that you will totally disregard your haves, oughts, needs, wants, or desires. What is important is to link what you *have* to be, do, or have to what you *love* to be, do, and have—either directly or via the oughts, needs, wants, desires, and choices in your life. Similarly, link your *oughts* to your loves—either directly or via your needs, wants, desires, and choices. Align and link your *needs* to your loves—either directly or via your wants, desires, and choices. Make sure you link your *wants* to your loves—either directly or via your desires and choices. Link your *desires* to your loves—directly or via your choices. Link all your *choices* to your loves.

Persevere in how and what you *have* to be, do, and have; so you can persevere at how and what you *ought* to be, do, and have; so you can persevere at how and what you *need* to be, do, and have; so you can persevere at how and what you *want* to be, do, and have; so you can persevere at how and what you *desire* to be, do, and have; so you can have a choice to persevere in *choosing* to be, do, and have how and what you love. You must fulfill some haves in order to graduate to your oughts, and some oughts to graduate to your needs, some needs to graduate to your wants, some wants to graduate to your desires, some desires to graduate to your choices, and some choices by graduating to your loves. Keep your haves, oughts, needs, wants, and desires to a minimum so you can feel free to choose your loves. Think of your purpose as a car, and keep the baggage to a minimum on the outside and inside, so your car is both light and aerodynamic.

If you wander off the path and make a mistake by omitting or committing what is not linked to your purpose, be gentle with yourself. Do not breed more fear and guilt by beating yourself up. Just realize that whatever it was, it was an experience that you needed at the time of the event. Get back on your feet and head toward what you love. Persevere in accepting your faults and polishing them smooth, and stay on purpose. You are now too focused on fulfilling your valuable mission in life to let transient events hold you down.

Persevere in the path of your most meaningful and highly valued intangible purpose. Persevere with total command of all your faculties and sustained, purposeful attention to the matter at hand, with unusual perception and protracted patience.

Persevere in holding your vision before you on the movie screen of your mind as you go about your daily activities. Persevere in affirming your affirmations as you rise and rest, until they mysteriously evolve into your words of power. Persevere in picturing, listening for, and feeling the balanced pros (+) and cons (−) in every endeavor, until you can feel them with love. Persevere in writing your loves, and your infatuations and resentments, with infinite detail on a daily basis. Persevere in acting as directly and economically as you can toward your purpose. Persevere in liberating and directing energy with order, as you act on the matter at hand. Persevere in present-now consciousness as you take action on the matter available. Persevere with an attitude of gratitude.

Persevere in realizing that you cannot make the best move in the absolute sense, and yet you can make the best move in the relative sense. Persevere in taking the best action in the relative sense while attempting to take the best action in the absolute sense, and persevere in allowing yourself to fall short of taking the best action in the absolute sense. Deciding *not* to take any purposeful action is a decision to stay in a rut, and anything in the universe that is not evolving on purpose is disintegrating in form. So which do you decide to choose now?

Some people will be drawn to you because of who you are, what you do, what you have, and what you say. Some will be repelled from you because of who you are, what you do, what you have, and what you say. Persevere on purpose and allow others to be who, what, and how they are, as they are.

Anyone who has stepped forward and chosen to follow the vertical path of purpose, affecting greater spheres of time and space, has encountered others who have criticized them with malice, irony, or envy. It is better to have the entire world against you than for you to be against the inspiration of the light of your Power on High. A Chinese proverb states, "One who cannot tolerate small ills cannot accomplish great things."

·Allow yourself to let people say what they say. Do not worry about their opinions.

Anyone's judgment directed at you may or may not have value. Listen and look with objective observation. Your inner power within knows. Listen to the inner voice with wisdom and understanding. Do not react to the reactions of others.

There is a power that is revealed in action, and there is a hidden power that is expressed in protecting the power of others. Confucius said, "The truly virtuous one . . . desiring to be established himself, seeks to establish others," and "The superior man honors the worthy and tolerates all men."

Simply act on purpose with certainty on your inspired mission. Persevere regardless of however many are in confederacy against you. Realize that to be great is to be misunderstood. Persevere in humbleness to your Power on High.

Persevere in purposeful, fulfilled, vital magnetism with indifference to pain and pleasure. Heracleitus said, "Know that war is common to all, and strife is justice [balance of polar opposites], and that all things come into being by strife."

Persevere though many curse, scorn, or mock you. Confucius said, "The man capable of governing is independent of public opinion."

Be purposefully steadfast and undisturbed, with powerfully unmovable determination as strong and solid as a rock. Be one of the few courageous people who leaves an immortal effect on our world by expanding your consciousness to stretch the borders of time and space, leading the many along toward your purpose.

Persevere in responding to life with unconditional love and gratitude for self, others, and your Power on High. Realize that you cannot respond for others. Each of us must respond to our own lives. Persevere in allowing others to have their evolution —without judgment, comment, or opinion.

Persevere in being judicial in making promises to please people. Ask yourself if pleasing another is linked to fulfilling your purpose in life. If the answer is no, then save yourself and others many relatively pointless cycles of infatuations and resentments, even if it means being resented in the short-term. Seek not to stir up resentments in others, but if you must choose between others resenting you and you resenting others, let others resent you. Persevere with great courage and accept solitude. It is the price you pay for greatness.

Persevere with an infinite capacity for tremendous pain and pleasure as you actualize your purposeful goals. Persevere in responding to life with unconditional love and gratitude every day. Persevere in persevering until, during, and ever after your co-creative masterpiece is manifest.

Persevere in studying what you love in detail and wonder. Dare to persevere with an intrepidity that nothing can check. Persevere with a will that cannot be broken. Will to persevere with a prudence that nothing can corrupt or intoxicate. Persevere in golden silence with what you know that you know that you know.

Persevere on purpose, doing what you do and being who you are with the awareness that many do not realize what you do, but that afterwards a few will understand. Persevere at breaking through the "limits" of your abilities imposed by genetics and environment as your intangible purpose guides you to choose the best action at any given time or place in space.

Persevere in adhering steadfastly to your purpose despite obstacles or setbacks. Persevere in steady, unswerving loyalty, constantly focused on your purpose. Persevere in devotion to the truth and actuality of your purpose. Persevere in giving yourself to virtue's cause.

There is an ancient saying, "Be thou wise, and fear not thy tribulations, for out of chaos is brought to birth a star." Let your light shine.

There is a way to actualize your values and you will certainly find it, so persevere unrelentingly. Persevere in finding the opportunity in every crisis, and realize that you have an abundant wealth of resources. Persevere in burning your one torch very brightly so you may manifest light in many.

Persevere with an intense desire to contribute to the purposeful good, virtue, and beauty of mankind — in greater spheres of time and space than most men and women conceive — and be rewarded greatly with a manifestation of significance and meaning that stands the test of time.

MANIFESTATION

- *Purpose* gives us our why.

- Clarity of *thought* gives us a path.

- *Vision* gives us our target.

- *Affirmation* leads us to a loving feeling for who we are, what we do, and what we have.

- *Feeling* leads us to magnetically attract the perfect people, places, ideas, and events.

- *Writing* is the first tangible step that leads us to action.

- *Action* is how we tangibly perform, to bring about what we love.

- *Energy* intensifies our action on the matter at hand.

- *Matter* is what we apply our action to.

- *Gratitude* is the pathway that opens our heart to the powerful flow of inspiration from on High, gifting us with greater purpose; purer thoughts; brighter, incredibly vivid vision; clearer, audible calling; stronger, unified love; infinitely more detailed writing; more intense action in the shortest time; higher-powered energy; and higher quality and quantity of matter.

✦ All of this births evermore gratitude, which drives you to purposefully *persevere*, and the cycle of manifesting continues infinitely.

Each complete cycle of the manifestation formula lifts us higher on the hierarchy of actualization. We move from the *have to* level, to the *ought to* level, to the *need to* level, to the *want to* level, to the *desire to* level, to the *choose to* level, to the *love to* level. Wherever you find yourself on this hierarchy of actualization (in each of the seven areas of your life), apply the manifestation formula to your life in its entirety, and allow yourself to raise your perception of self-worth by raising yourself up on the vertical plane of purposeful manifestation now.

You do not have to decide to wake up and consciously work the manifestation formula now. But if you were to stop and consider your choices, you might ask yourself a question such as, Am I responding to life, or is life responding to my omission to respond? Realize that your life events will seem to call, nudge, prod, shake, shove, hit, and kick you until you finally wake up and respond to your life with vision, inspiration, and purpose.

Your Power on High is infinitely loving and magnanimous. You choose to climb the vertical path of purpose or to leave the path to bump your head in the shadows of the light of the Power on High. The light from on High expressed in universal principles may seem a ruthless taskmaster, a teacher who will stop at nothing to raise your consciousness to purposeful, uncharged love and gratitude. Universal law is the impartial, uncharged, omnipotent force ever reminding you of your choice to remain at the center of the laser point of Light from on High, or to steer adrift into the dark night of the gradient shadows of the light and experience the bipolar existence of separation.

The grander your purpose, the more focused your thought, the more vivid your vision, and the more powerful your affirmative words. The grander your purpose, the greater your magnetic feeling of love, the more detailed your written grand plan, and the more powerfully inspired your actions. The grander your purpose, the more organized and prioritized your energy, the more you make of the matter at hand, and the more matter you will find available to make more of. The grander your purpose, the greater your gratitude for each goal and objective achieved, the more determined your perseverance, and the grander your manifestation.

The more clear and focused your thought, the more vivid your vision, the more audible your calling, and the more powerful and magnetic your feeling of love. The more clear and focused your thought, the more detailed, descriptive, and accurate your written memories and imagination of who you are, where you came from, where you are going, and why you are here; and the more direct your actions toward who, what, and how you love. The more clear and focused your thought, the more energy you liberate and direct to take incredible action now; the more details you appreciate about the matter at hand; and the more gratitude you experience for what was, what is, and what will be. The more clear and focused your thought, the more deliberate your perseverance, the more meaningful and significant your purpose, and the more distinct your manifestation.

The more brightly vivid and intensely animated your vision, the louder the calling of your words of power, and the more intense the feeling of love for where you come from, who you are, why you are here now, and where you are going in your incredibly purposeful life. The more brightly vivid and intensely animated your vision, the more compelled you feel to immediately write it down in time and space, the more you naturally find yourself taking intense action immediately, and the more directly your energy flows toward manifesting your vision. The more brightly vivid and intensely animated your vision, the more easily the matter at hand is mysteriously transformed into who, what, and how you envision; the more gratitude and inspiration you express and receive; and the more easily you persevere. The more brightly vivid and intensely animated your vision, the greater the significance and meaning of your purpose; the more focused and clear the thoughts you express; and the more powerful your manifestation.

The more audible the calling in your affirmative words of power, the more powerfully magnetic your feeling of love, the stronger your urge to write it down immediately in fine detail, and the more effective your action steps to bring it to pass. The more audible the calling in your affirmative words of power, the more available and focused your energy, the higher quality and greater quantity of the matter you attract at hand, and the more gratitude you express to your Power on High. The more audible the calling in your affirmative words of power, the more certain you are of your purpose, the more clear and focused your thought, the more aligned you are with your vivid vision, and the greater your manifestation.

The more powerful the magnetic feeling of love you exude, the more inspired your written message, the more ordered your actions, and the more uplifting your energy, applied toward your purposeful actions. The more powerful the magnetic feeling of love you exude, the higher the order of the purposeful matter you attract and move toward, the greater the magnitude of gratitude you express, and the more easily you naturally find yourself persevering. The more powerful the magnetic feeling of love you feel, the more inspiring your purpose, the more present-now consciousness in your thoughts, the more inspiring your vision, and the louder your calling. The more powerful the magnetic feeling of love you feel, the more perfect your manifestation.

The finer the detail you remember and imagine as you write them down in time and space, the more freedom and courage you have to take action now, and the more energy you liberate toward your purpose. The finer the detail you write about who, what, and how you love, the finer the matter you attract and move toward. The finer the detail you write about the past with symmetry, proportion, and order, the more gratitude you express, the more inspired you are by the message from on High, and the finer the detail you map for your future as you become simultaneously present with past and future now. The finer the detail in your written road map to your purposeful source, the greater your certainty of persevering, the more your purpose is revealed, and the greater and clearer your thoughts. The finer the detail in your writing, the more brightly vivid and intensely animated your vision, the greater your calling, and the greater your love for who, what, and how you are destined to be, do, and have. The finer the detail in your writing, the more detail you receive in your manifestation.

The more purposeful and efficient your actions, the more energy you focus, and the more mass of the matter you love is accumulated. The more action steps you take, the more you find to be grateful for. The wiser the action, the greater the perseverance. The more intentional your action, the closer you get to your purpose. The more deliberate your action, the clearer your thought. The greater the action you accomplish, the more your vision expands. The greater the action you accomplish, the greater your conviction in your affirmative words of power. The greater the purposeful action you accomplish, the more love you feel for your Power on High. The more you accomplish, the more you find yourself designing your life by writing your vision, inspiration, and purpose in time and space. The more action you take, the more you manifest.

The more energy you purposefully focus toward the matter at hand, the higher the quality of matter you attract, move toward, and encounter as the perfect people, places, and things. The more purposeful energy you wisely direct, the more inspiration you receive, the more the gratitude you express, and the more easily you naturally find yourself persevering. The more intense the energy you wisely direct, the more closely you approach your purpose, the greater your clarity of thought, the more fulfilled your vision, and the more purposefully succinct your affirmative words of power. The more intense the energy you wisely direct, the greater the magnetic feeling of love you experience for who, what, and how you love to be, do, and have; the finer the details in your writing within time and space; the greater the immediate action you take now; and the more powerful your manifestation.

The higher the quality of matter you attract and move toward, the more inspiration and gratitude you experience, the more inspired you are to persevere, and the closer you get to fulfilling your purpose. The higher the quality of matter you attract and move toward, the more certain your thoughts, the more fulfilled your vision, and the more your vision grows. The higher the quality of matter you attract and move toward, the more fulfilled your words of power, the more powerful the vibration of your words, and the more fulfilled you feel. The higher the quality and quantity of matter you experience, the more actualized your written vision becomes, the more your actions are rewarded, and the more actions you find yourself taking. The higher the quality of matter you experience, the more energy you receive and give, flowing from above, down, and inside you, and flowing out to form your manifestation. As you experience higher quality and quantity of matter, you find yourself reaching an energetic point of critical mass, infinitely manifesting who, what, and how you love to be, do, and have.

The greater your gratitude, the more easily you find yourself persevering, the more your purpose is confirmed and revealed, the clearer your thought, the more vividly bright and animated your vision, and the more power in the words of your calling. The greater the love and gratitude you express, the more inspiration and love you receive, the more inspired your writing, and the greater your ability to immediately act on who, what, and how you love to be, do, and have. The greater the gratitude you experience, the more energy you give and receive, the higher the quality and quantity of matter you receive, and the greater your manifestation.

The greater your perseverance, the more your true purpose unfolds and is fulfilled, the more powerful your thought becomes, and the more your vision is fulfilled and expanded. The greater your perseverance, the greater the meaning and power of your words, and the more your love grows for who you are, where you came from, where you are going, and why you are here now. The greater your perseverance, the greater your writing becomes, the more powerful your actions become, and the more inspired you feel. The greater your perseverance, the more gratitude you experience for who you are, what you do, and what you have, and the greater your manifestation.

Purposefully focus your unified thought on your vision. Affirm your vision and feel it with the power of love. Write your loves in time and space and take action with energy on the matter at hand. Be eternally grateful for what was, what is, and what shall be. Persevere as the tangible world and the intangible universe conform and conspire to manifest your success now. Make gratitude and joy your primary prayer. Make inspiration your meditation, as you know that you know that you know that the Power on High is the source of your supply, and the power within you is the way. Your true needs, wants, desires, and loves are met within every moment of time and point of space as you show up and stand up on the vertical plane.

The Omnipotent and Omniscient Presence which guides earth, the other planets, our sun, the 200-billion-plus stars of our galaxy, the billions of stars in the billions of galaxies that make up our universe, and each universe that makes up the pleuriverse—causing every one of those star-suns to shine and every one of the planets to orbit about each of those star-suns —watches over you now.

Persevere with an intense desire to contribute to the purpose-ful good, the virtue, and the beauty of mankind—in greater spheres of time and space than most men and women conceive —and be rewarded greatly with a manifestation of significance and meaning that stands the test of time. From star dust you have come and to star dust you will return, so let your light shine brightly with vision, inspiration, and purpose today.

PAR NEFER

APPENDIX

COMMUNICATION ENHANCEMENT FORM

Perception of symmetry, proportion, and order leads us to truth.
The truth builds love and acceptance.

(+) Column 1: Positives or "goods." The omissions or commissions that you like and/or with which you are infatuated. ✦ The positive qualities, habits, character or personality traits you admire. ✦ Things that have attracted you to them. ✦ Things you would praise.	(+) Column 2: Episodes where and when you have been or done the same, somewhere in the seven areas of life. Think of any past or present person, place, thing, idea, or event.
Handsome, nice hair	I have nice smile and eyes
Strong faith, believes in God	I too am faithful to God
Polite, charming, educated	I have been told I have charisma
Makes a lot of money	I support my family and society
Was there for me	I have been there for Jo
Popular in school	I was popular at work
Good relationship with father	I have a good relationship with my brother

EXAMPLE

*When positives outweigh negatives, you become attracted and infatuated. When negatives outweigh positives, you become repelled and resentful. When positives equal negatives (equal in degree, kind, magnitude, quantity, and quality), they **collapse** into each other, enlightening*

For free copies of this form, call (713) 334-0777 or write to:
Dr. Richard Bellamy, 2400 Augusta Drive, Suite 210, Houston, TX 77057

Person filling out form: _____

Person, place, thing, idea, or event attracted to or repelled from:

_____

The seven areas of life are:
physical, spiritual, mental, career, financial, family, and social.

(–) Column 3: Negatives or "bads." The omissions or commissions that you dislike and/or resent. ✦ The negative qualities, habits, character or personality traits you despise. ✦ Things that have repelled you from them. ✦ Things you would reprimand.	(–) Column 4: Episodes where and when you have been or done the same, somewhere in the seven areas of life. Think of any past or present person, place, thing, idea, or event.
Let me down financially	I let Linda down emotionally in relationship
Overweight	I have been weighed down physically and socially
Wastes my time	I wasted my parents' money
Incompetent repairing household problems	I was incompetent with managing my time
Tells me how to spend my money	I tell people what to do in their lives
Wasn't there for me	I have not been there for Susan
Shut me out	I shut Lori out

EXAMPLE

you to become accepting and loving. To love some person, place, thing, idea, or event is to accept what you like and dislike about it. Communication is maximized in the love state. Whatever you are able to love builds love in you. People, places, things, ideas, and events are reflections of you.

COMMUNICATION ENHANCEMENT FORM

Perception of symmetry, proportion, and order leads us to truth.
The truth builds love and acceptance.

(+) Column 1: Positives or "goods." The omissions or commissions that you like and/or with which you are infatuated. ✦ The positive qualities, habits, character or personality traits you admire. ✦ Things that have attracted you to them. ✦ Things you would praise.	(+) Column 2: Episodes where and when you have been or done the same, somewhere in the seven areas of life. Think of any past or present person, place, thing, idea, or event.

*When positives outweigh negatives, you become attracted and infatuated. When negatives outweigh positives, you become repelled and resentful. When positives equal negatives (equal in degree, kind, magnitude, quantity, and quality), they **collapse** into each other, enlightening*

For free copies of this form, call (713) 334-0777 or write to:
Dr. Richard Bellamy, 2400 Augusta Drive, Suite 210, Houston, TX 77057

Person filling out form: _____

Person, place, thing, idea, or event attracted to or repelled from:

_____

The seven areas of life are:
physical, spiritual, mental, career, financial, family, and social.

(–) Column 3: Negatives or "bads." The omissions or commissions that you dislike and/or resent. ✦ The negative qualities, habits, character or personality traits you despise. ✦ Things that have repelled you from them. ✦ Things you would reprimand.	(–) Column 4: Episodes where and when you have been or done the same, somewhere in the seven areas of life. Think of any past or present person, place, thing, idea, or event.

you to become accepting and loving. To love some person, place, thing, idea, or event is to accept what you like and dislike about it. Communication is maximized in the love state. Whatever you are able to love builds love in you. People, places, things, ideas, and events are reflections of you.

COMMUNICATION ENHANCEMENT FORM

Perception of symmetry, proportion, and order leads us to truth.
The truth builds love and acceptance.

(+) Column 1: Positives or "goods." The omissions or commissions that you like and/or with which you are infatuated. ✦ The positive qualities, habits, character or personality traits you admire. ✦ Things that have attracted you to them. ✦ Things you would praise.	(+) Column 2: Episodes where and when you have been or done the same, somewhere in the seven areas of life. Think of any past or present person, place, thing, idea, or event.

*When positives outweigh negatives, you become attracted and infatuated. When negatives outweigh positives, you become repelled and resentful. When positives equal negatives (equal in degree, kind, magnitude, quantity, and quality), they **collapse** into each other, enlightening*

For free copies of this form, call (713) 334-0777 or write to:
Dr. Richard Bellamy, 2400 Augusta Drive, Suite 210, Houston, TX 77057

Person filling out form: _____

Person, place, thing, idea, or event attracted to or repelled from:

_____

The seven areas of life are:
physical, spiritual, mental, career, financial, family, and social.

(–) Column 3: Negatives or "bads."	(–) Column 4:
The omissions or commissions that you dislike and/or resent. ✦ The negative qualities, habits, character or personality traits you despise. ✦ Things that have repelled you from them. ✦ Things you would reprimand.	Episodes where and when you have been or done the same, somewhere in the seven areas of life. Think of any past or present person, place, thing, idea, or event.

you to become accepting and loving. To love some person, place, thing, idea, or event is to accept what you like and dislike about it. Communication is maximized in the love state. Whatever you are able to love builds love in you. People, places, things, ideas, and events are reflections of you.

COMMUNICATION ENHANCEMENT FORM

Perception of symmetry, proportion, and order leads us to truth.
The truth builds love and acceptance.

(+) Column 1: Positives or "goods." The omissions or commissions that you like and/or with which you are infatuated. ✦ The positive qualities, habits, character or personality traits you admire. ✦ Things that have attracted you to them. ✦ Things you would praise.	(+) Column 2: Episodes where and when you have been or done the same, somewhere in the seven areas of life. Think of any past or present person, place, thing, idea, or event.

*When positives outweigh negatives, you become attracted and infatuated. When negatives outweigh positives, you become repelled and resentful. When positives equal negatives (equal in degree, kind, magnitude, quantity, and quality), they **collapse** into each other, enlightening*

For free copies of this form, call (713) 334-0777 or write to:
Dr. Richard Bellamy, 2400 Augusta Drive, Suite 210, Houston, TX 77057

Person filling out form: _____

Person, place, thing, idea, or event attracted to or repelled from:

_____

The seven areas of life are:
physical, spiritual, mental, career, financial, family, and social.

(–) Column 3: Negatives or "bads." The omissions or commissions that you dislike and/or resent. ✦ The negative qualities, habits, character or personality traits you despise. ✦ Things that have repelled you from them. ✦ Things you would reprimand.	(–) Column 4: Episodes where and when you have been or done the same, somewhere in the seven areas of life. Think of any past or present person, place, thing, idea, or event.

you to become accepting and loving. To love some person, place, thing, idea, or event is to accept what you like and dislike about it. Communication is maximized in the love state. Whatever you are able to love builds love in you. People, places, things, ideas, and events are reflections of you.

COMMUNICATION ENHANCEMENT FORM

Perception of symmetry, proportion, and order leads us to truth.
The truth builds love and acceptance.

(+) Column 1: Positives or "goods." The omissions or commissions that you like and/or with which you are infatuated. ✦ The positive qualities, habits, character or personality traits you admire. ✦ Things that have attracted you to them. ✦ Things you would praise.	(+) Column 2: Episodes where and when you have been or done the same, somewhere in the seven areas of life. Think of any past or present person, place, thing, idea, or event.

*When positives outweigh negatives, you become attracted and infatuated. When negatives outweigh positives, you become repelled and resentful. When positives equal negatives (equal in degree, kind, magnitude, quantity, and quality), they **collapse** into each other, enlightening*

For free copies of this form, call (713) 334-0777 or write to:
Dr. Richard Bellamy, 2400 Augusta Drive, Suite 210, Houston, TX 77057

Person filling out form: _____

Person, place, thing, idea, or event attracted to or repelled from:

_____

The seven areas of life are:
physical, spiritual, mental, career, financial, family, and social.

(–) Column 3: Negatives or "bads." The omissions or commissions that you dislike and/or resent. ✦ The negative qualities, habits, character or personality traits you despise. ✦ Things that have repelled you from them. ✦ Things you would reprimand.	(–) Column 4: Episodes where and when you have been or done the same, somewhere in the seven areas of life. Think of any past or present person, place, thing, idea, or event.

you to become accepting and loving. To love some person, place, thing, idea, or event is to accept what you like and dislike about it. Communication is maximized in the love state. Whatever you are able to love builds love in you. People, places, things, ideas, and events are reflections of you.

COMMUNICATION ENHANCEMENT FORM

Perception of symmetry, proportion, and order leads us to truth.
The truth builds love and acceptance.

(+) Column 1: Positives or "goods." The omissions or commissions that you like and/or with which you are infatuated. ✦ The positive qualities, habits, character or personality traits you admire. ✦ Things that have attracted you to them. ✦ Things you would praise.	(+) Column 2: Episodes where and when you have been or done the same, somewhere in the seven areas of life. Think of any past or present person, place, thing, idea, or event.

*When positives outweigh negatives, you become attracted and infatuated. When negatives outweigh positives, you become repelled and resentful. When positives equal negatives (equal in degree, kind, magnitude, quantity, and quality), they **collapse** into each other, enlightening*

For free copies of this form, call (713) 334-0777 or write to:
Dr. Richard Bellamy, 2400 Augusta Drive, Suite 210, Houston, TX 77057

Person filling out form: _____

Person, place, thing, idea, or event attracted to or repelled from:

_____

The seven areas of life are:
physical, spiritual, mental, career, financial, family, and social.

(–) Column 3: Negatives or "bads." The omissions or commissions that you dislike and/or resent. ✦ The negative qualities, habits, character or personality traits you despise. ✦ Things that have repelled you from them. ✦ Things you would reprimand.	(–) Column 4: Episodes where and when you have been or done the same, somewhere in the seven areas of life. Think of any past or present person, place, thing, idea, or event.

you to become accepting and loving. To love some person, place, thing, idea, or event is to accept what you like and dislike about it. Communication is maximized in the love state. Whatever you are able to love builds love in you. People, places, things, ideas, and events are reflections of you.

COMMUNICATION ENHANCEMENT FORM

Perception of symmetry, proportion, and order leads us to truth.
The truth builds love and acceptance.

(+) Column 1: Positives or "goods." The omissions or commissions that you like and/or with which you are infatuated. ✦ The positive qualities, habits, character or personality traits you admire. ✦ Things that have attracted you to them. ✦ Things you would praise.	(+) Column 2: Episodes where and when you have been or done the same, somewhere in the seven areas of life. Think of any past or present person, place, thing, idea, or event.

*When positives outweigh negatives, you become attracted and infatuated. When negatives outweigh positives, you become repelled and resentful. When positives equal negatives (equal in degree, kind, magnitude, quantity, and quality), they **collapse** into each other, enlightening*

For free copies of this form, call (713) 334-0777 or write to:
Dr. Richard Bellamy, 2400 Augusta Drive, Suite 210, Houston, TX 77057

Person filling out form: _____

Person, place, thing, idea, or event attracted to or repelled from:

_____

The seven areas of life are:
physical, spiritual, mental, career, financial, family, and social.

(–) Column 3: Negatives or "bads." The omissions or commissions that you dislike and/or resent. ✦ The negative qualities, habits, character or personality traits you despise. ✦ Things that have repelled you from them. ✦ Things you would reprimand.	(–) Column 4: Episodes where and when you have been or done the same, somewhere in the seven areas of life. Think of any past or present person, place, thing, idea, or event.

you to become accepting and loving. To love some person, place, thing, idea, or event is to accept what you like and dislike about it. Communication is maximized in the love state. Whatever you are able to love builds love in you. People, places, things, ideas, and events are reflections of you.

COMMUNICATION ENHANCEMENT FORM

Perception of symmetry, proportion, and order leads us to truth.
The truth builds love and acceptance.

(+) Column 1: Positives or "goods." The omissions or commissions that you like and/or with which you are infatuated. ◆ The positive qualities, habits, character or personality traits you admire. ◆ Things that have attracted you to them. ◆ Things you would praise.	(+) Column 2: Episodes where and when you have been or done the same, somewhere in the seven areas of life. Think of any past or present person, place, thing, idea, or event.

*When positives outweigh negatives, you become attracted and infatuated. When negatives outweigh positives, you become repelled and resentful. When positives equal negatives (equal in degree, kind, magnitude, quantity, and quality), they **collapse** into each other, enlightening*

For free copies of this form, call (713) 334-0777 or write to:
Dr. Richard Bellamy, 2400 Augusta Drive, Suite 210, Houston, TX 77057

Person filling out form: _____

Person, place, thing, idea, or event attracted to or repelled from:

_____

The seven areas of life are:
physical, spiritual, mental, career, financial, family, and social.

(–) Column 3: Negatives or "bads." The omissions or commissions that you dislike and/or resent. ✦ The negative qualities, habits, character or personality traits you despise. ✦ Things that have repelled you from them. ✦ Things you would reprimand.	(–) Column 4: Episodes where and when you have been or done the same, somewhere in the seven areas of life. Think of any past or present person, place, thing, idea, or event.

you to become accepting and loving. To love some person, place, thing, idea, or event is to accept what you like and dislike about it. Communication is maximized in the love state. Whatever you are able to love builds love in you. People, places, things, ideas, and events are reflections of you.

COMMUNICATION ENHANCEMENT FORM

Perception of symmetry, proportion, and order leads us to truth.
The truth builds love and acceptance.

(+) Column 1: Positives or "goods." The omissions or commissions that you like and/or with which you are infatuated. ◆ The positive qualities, habits, character or personality traits you admire. ◆ Things that have attracted you to them. ◆ Things you would praise.	(+) Column 2: Episodes where and when you have been or done the same, somewhere in the seven areas of life. Think of any past or present person, place, thing, idea, or event.

*When positives outweigh negatives, you become attracted and infatuated. When negatives outweigh positives, you become repelled and resentful. When positives equal negatives (equal in degree, kind, magnitude, quantity, and quality), they **collapse** into each other, enlightening*

For free copies of this form, call (713) 334-0777 or write to:
Dr. Richard Bellamy, 2400 Augusta Drive, Suite 210, Houston, TX 77057

Person filling out form: _____

Person, place, thing, idea, or event attracted to or repelled from:

_____

The seven areas of life are:
physical, spiritual, mental, career, financial, family, and social.

(–) Column 3: Negatives or "bads." The omissions or commissions that you dislike and/or resent. ✦ The negative qualities, habits, character or personality traits you despise. ✦ Things that have repelled you from them. ✦ Things you would reprimand.	(–) Column 4: Episodes where and when you have been or done the same, somewhere in the seven areas of life. Think of any past or present person, place, thing, idea, or event.

you to become accepting and loving. To love some person, place, thing, idea, or event is to accept what you like and dislike about it. Communication is maximized in the love state. Whatever you are able to love builds love in you. People, places, things, ideas, and events are reflections of you.

COMMUNICATION ENHANCEMENT FORM

Perception of symmetry, proportion, and order leads us to truth.
The truth builds love and acceptance.

(+) Column 1: Positives or "goods." The omissions or commissions that you like and/or with which you are infatuated. ✦ The positive qualities, habits, character or personality traits you admire. ✦ Things that have attracted you to them. ✦ Things you would praise.	(+) Column 2: Episodes where and when you have been or done the same, somewhere in the seven areas of life. Think of any past or present person, place, thing, idea, or event.

*When positives outweigh negatives, you become attracted and infatuated. When negatives outweigh positives, you become repelled and resentful. When positives equal negatives (equal in degree, kind, magnitude, quantity, and quality), they **collapse** into each other, enlightening*

For free copies of this form, call (713) 334-0777 or write to:
Dr. Richard Bellamy, 2400 Augusta Drive, Suite 210, Houston, TX 77057

Person filling out form: _____

Person, place, thing, idea, or event attracted to or repelled from:

_____

The seven areas of life are:
physical, spiritual, mental, career, financial, family, and social.

(–) Column 3: Negatives or "bads." The omissions or commissions that you dislike and/or resent. ✦ The negative qualities, habits, character or personality traits you despise. ✦ Things that have repelled you from them. ✦ Things you would reprimand.	(–) Column 4: Episodes where and when you have been or done the same, somewhere in the seven areas of life. Think of any past or present person, place, thing, idea, or event.

you to become accepting and loving. To love some person, place, thing, idea, or event is to accept what you like and dislike about it. Communication is maximized in the love state. Whatever you are able to love builds love in you. People, places, things, ideas, and events are reflections of you.

COMMUNICATION ENHANCEMENT FORM

Perception of symmetry, proportion, and order leads us to truth.
The truth builds love and acceptance.

(+) Column 1: Positives or "goods." The omissions or commissions that you like and/or with which you are infatuated. ✦ The positive qualities, habits, character or personality traits you admire. ✦ Things that have attracted you to them. ✦ Things you would praise.	(+) Column 2: Episodes where and when you have been or done the same, somewhere in the seven areas of life. Think of any past or present person, place, thing, idea, or event.

*When positives outweigh negatives, you become attracted and infatuated. When negatives outweigh positives, you become repelled and resentful. When positives equal negatives (equal in degree, kind, magnitude, quantity, and quality), they **collapse** into each other, enlightening*

For free copies of this form, call (713) 334-0777 or write to:
Dr. Richard Bellamy, 2400 Augusta Drive, Suite 210, Houston, TX 77057

Person filling out form: _____

Person, place, thing, idea, or event attracted to or repelled from:

_____

The seven areas of life are:
physical, spiritual, mental, career, financial, family, and social.

(–) Column 3: Negatives or "bads." The omissions or commissions that you dislike and/or resent. ✦ The negative qualities, habits, character or personality traits you despise. ✦ Things that have repelled you from them. ✦ Things you would reprimand.	(–) Column 4: Episodes where and when you have been or done the same, somewhere in the seven areas of life. Think of any past or present person, place, thing, idea, or event.

you to become accepting and loving. To love some person, place, thing, idea, or event is to accept what you like and dislike about it. Communication is maximized in the love state. Whatever you are able to love builds love in you. People, places, things, ideas, and events are reflections of you.

COMMUNICATION ENHANCEMENT FORM

Perception of symmetry, proportion, and order leads us to truth.
The truth builds love and acceptance.

(+) Column 1: Positives or "goods." The omissions or commissions that you like and/or with which you are infatuated. ✦ The positive qualities, habits, character or personality traits you admire. ✦ Things that have attracted you to them. ✦ Things you would praise.	(+) Column 2: Episodes where and when you have been or done the same, somewhere in the seven areas of life. Think of any past or present person, place, thing, idea, or event.

*When positives outweigh negatives, you become attracted and infatuated. When negatives outweigh positives, you become repelled and resentful. When positives equal negatives (equal in degree, kind, magnitude, quantity, and quality), they **collapse** into each other, enlightening*

For free copies of this form, call (713) 334-0777 or write to:
Dr. Richard Bellamy, 2400 Augusta Drive, Suite 210, Houston, TX 77057

Person filling out form: _____

Person, place, thing, idea, or event attracted to or repelled from:

_____

The seven areas of life are:
physical, spiritual, mental, career, financial, family, and social.

(–) Column 3: Negatives or "bads." The omissions or commissions that you dislike and/or resent. ✦ The negative qualities, habits, character or personality traits you despise. ✦ Things that have repelled you from them. ✦ Things you would reprimand.	(–) Column 4: Episodes where and when you have been or done the same, somewhere in the seven areas of life. Think of any past or present person, place, thing, idea, or event.

you to become accepting and loving. To love some person, place, thing, idea, or event is to accept what you like and dislike about it. Communication is maximized in the love state. Whatever you are able to love builds love in you. People, places, things, ideas, and events are reflections of you.

COMMUNICATION ENHANCEMENT FORM

Perception of symmetry, proportion, and order leads us to truth.
The truth builds love and acceptance.

(+) Column 1: Positives or "goods." The omissions or commissions that you like and/or with which you are infatuated. ♦ The positive qualities, habits, character or personality traits you admire. ♦ Things that have attracted you to them. ♦ Things you would praise.	(+) Column 2: Episodes where and when you have been or done the same, somewhere in the seven areas of life. Think of any past or present person, place, thing, idea, or event.

*When positives outweigh negatives, you become attracted and infatuated. When negatives outweigh positives, you become repelled and resentful. When positives equal negatives (equal in degree, kind, magnitude, quantity, and quality), they **collapse** into each other, enlightening*

For free copies of this form, call (713) 334-0777 or write to:
Dr. Richard Bellamy, 2400 Augusta Drive, Suite 210, Houston, TX 77057

Person filling out form: _____

Person, place, thing, idea, or event attracted to or repelled from:

_____

The seven areas of life are:
physical, spiritual, mental, career, financial, family, and social.

(–) Column 3: Negatives or "bads." The omissions or commissions that you dislike and/or resent. ✦ The negative qualities, habits, character or personality traits you despise. ✦ Things that have repelled you from them. ✦ Things you would reprimand.	(–) Column 4: Episodes where and when you have been or done the same, somewhere in the seven areas of life. Think of any past or present person, place, thing, idea, or event.

you to become accepting and loving. To love some person, place, thing, idea, or event is to accept what you like and dislike about it. Communication is maximized in the love state. Whatever you are able to love builds love in you. People, places, things, ideas, and events are reflections of you.

COMMUNICATION ENHANCEMENT FORM

Perception of symmetry, proportion, and order leads us to truth.
The truth builds love and acceptance.

(+) Column 1: Positives or "goods." The omissions or commissions that you like and/or with which you are infatuated. ✦ The positive qualities, habits, character or personality traits you admire. ✦ Things that have attracted you to them. ✦ Things you would praise.	(+) Column 2: Episodes where and when you have been or done the same, somewhere in the seven areas of life. Think of any past or present person, place, thing, idea, or event.

*When positives outweigh negatives, you become attracted and infatuated. When negatives outweigh positives, you become repelled and resentful. When positives equal negatives (equal in degree, kind, magnitude, quantity, and quality), they **collapse** into each other, enlightening*

For free copies of this form, call (713) 334-0777 or write to:
Dr. Richard Bellamy, 2400 Augusta Drive, Suite 210, Houston, TX 77057

Person filling out form: _____

Person, place, thing, idea, or event attracted to or repelled from:

_____

The seven areas of life are:
physical, spiritual, mental, career, financial, family, and social.

(–) Column 3: Negatives or "bads." The omissions or commissions that you dislike and/or resent. ✦ The negative qualities, habits, character or personality traits you despise. ✦ Things that have repelled you from them. ✦ Things you would reprimand.	(–) Column 4: Episodes where and when you have been or done the same, somewhere in the seven areas of life. Think of any past or present person, place, thing, idea, or event.

you to become accepting and loving. To love some person, place, thing, idea, or event is to accept what you like and dislike about it. Communication is maximized in the love state. Whatever you are able to love builds love in you. People, places, things, ideas, and events are reflections of you.

COMMUNICATION ENHANCEMENT FORM

Perception of symmetry, proportion, and order leads us to truth.
The truth builds love and acceptance.

(+) Column 1: Positives or "goods." The omissions or commissions that you like and/or with which you are infatuated. ✦ The positive qualities, habits, character or personality traits you admire. ✦ Things that have attracted you to them. ✦ Things you would praise.	(+) Column 2: Episodes where and when you have been or done the same, somewhere in the seven areas of life. Think of any past or present person, place, thing, idea, or event.

*When positives outweigh negatives, you become attracted and infatuated. When negatives outweigh positives, you become repelled and resentful. When positives equal negatives (equal in degree, kind, magnitude, quantity, and quality), they **collapse** into each other, enlightening*

For free copies of this form, call (713) 334-0777 or write to:
Dr. Richard Bellamy, 2400 Augusta Drive, Suite 210, Houston, TX 77057

Person filling out form: _____

Person, place, thing, idea, or event attracted to or repelled from:

_____

The seven areas of life are:
physical, spiritual, mental, career, financial, family, and social.

(–) Column 3: Negatives or "bads." The omissions or commissions that you dislike and/or resent. ✦ The negative qualities, habits, character or personality traits you despise. ✦ Things that have repelled you from them. ✦ Things you would reprimand.	(–) Column 4: Episodes where and when you have been or done the same, somewhere in the seven areas of life. Think of any past or present person, place, thing, idea, or event.

you to become accepting and loving. To love some person, place, thing, idea, or event is to accept what you like and dislike about it. Communication is maximized in the love state. Whatever you are able to love builds love in you. People, places, things, ideas, and events are reflections of you.

COMMUNICATION ENHANCEMENT FORM

Perception of symmetry, proportion, and order leads us to truth.
The truth builds love and acceptance.

(+) Column 1: Positives or "goods." The omissions or commissions that you like and/or with which you are infatuated. ✦ The positive qualities, habits, character or personality traits you admire. ✦ Things that have attracted you to them. ✦ Things you would praise.	(+) Column 2: Episodes where and when you have been or done the same, somewhere in the seven areas of life. Think of any past or present person, place, thing, idea, or event.

*When positives outweigh negatives, you become attracted and infatuated. When negatives outweigh positives, you become repelled and resentful. When positives equal negatives (equal in degree, kind, magnitude, quantity, and quality), they **collapse** into each other, enlightening*

For free copies of this form, call (713) 334-0777 or write to:
Dr. Richard Bellamy, 2400 Augusta Drive, Suite 210, Houston, TX 77057

Person filling out form: _____

Person, place, thing, idea, or event attracted to or repelled from:

_____

The seven areas of life are:
physical, spiritual, mental, career, financial, family, and social.

(–) Column 3: Negatives or "bads." The omissions or commissions that you dislike and/or resent. ✦ The negative qualities, habits, character or personality traits you despise. ✦ Things that have repelled you from them. ✦ Things you would reprimand.	(–) Column 4: Episodes where and when you have been or done the same, somewhere in the seven areas of life. Think of any past or present person, place, thing, idea, or event.

you to become accepting and loving. To love some person, place, thing, idea, or event is to accept what you like and dislike about it. Communication is maximized in the love state. Whatever you are able to love builds love in you. People, places, things, ideas, and events are reflections of you.

COMMUNICATION ENHANCEMENT FORM

Perception of symmetry, proportion, and order leads us to truth.
The truth builds love and acceptance.

(+) Column 1: Positives or "goods." The omissions or commissions that you like and/or with which you are infatuated. ✦ The positive qualities, habits, character or personality traits you admire. ✦ Things that have attracted you to them. ✦ Things you would praise.	(+) Column 2: Episodes where and when you have been or done the same, somewhere in the seven areas of life. Think of any past or present person, place, thing, idea, or event.

*When positives outweigh negatives, you become attracted and infatuated. When negatives outweigh positives, you become repelled and resentful. When positives equal negatives (equal in degree, kind, magnitude, quantity, and quality), they **collapse** into each other, enlightening*

For free copies of this form, call (713) 334-0777 or write to:
Dr. Richard Bellamy, 2400 Augusta Drive, Suite 210, Houston, TX 77057

Person filling out form: _____

Person, place, thing, idea, or event attracted to or repelled from:

_____

The seven areas of life are:
physical, spiritual, mental, career, financial, family, and social.

(–) Column 3: Negatives or "bads." The omissions or commissions that you dislike and/or resent. ✦ The negative qualities, habits, character or personality traits you despise. ✦ Things that have repelled you from them. ✦ Things you would reprimand.	(–) Column 4: Episodes where and when you have been or done the same, somewhere in the seven areas of life. Think of any past or present person, place, thing, idea, or event.

you to become accepting and loving. To love some person, place, thing, idea, or event is to accept what you like and dislike about it. Communication is maximized in the love state. Whatever you are able to love builds love in you. People, places, things, ideas, and events are reflections of you.

COMMUNICATION ENHANCEMENT FORM

Perception of symmetry, proportion, and order leads us to truth.
The truth builds love and acceptance.

(+) Column 1: Positives or "goods." The omissions or commissions that you like and/or with which you are infatuated. ✦ The positive qualities, habits, character or personality traits you admire. ✦ Things that have attracted you to them. ✦ Things you would praise.	(+) Column 2: Episodes where and when you have been or done the same, somewhere in the seven areas of life. Think of any past or present person, place, thing, idea, or event.

*When positives outweigh negatives, you become attracted and infatuated. When negatives outweigh positives, you become repelled and resentful. When positives equal negatives (equal in degree, kind, magnitude, quantity, and quality), they **collapse** into each other, enlightening*

For free copies of this form, call (713) 334-0777 or write to:
Dr. Richard Bellamy, 2400 Augusta Drive, Suite 210, Houston, TX 77057

Person filling out form: _____

Person, place, thing, idea, or event attracted to or repelled from:

_____

The seven areas of life are:
physical, spiritual, mental, career, financial, family, and social.

(–) Column 3: Negatives or "bads." The omissions or commissions that you dislike and/or resent. ✦ The negative qualities, habits, character or personality traits you despise. ✦ Things that have repelled you from them. ✦ Things you would reprimand.	(–) Column 4: Episodes where and when you have been or done the same, somewhere in the seven areas of life. Think of any past or present person, place, thing, idea, or event.

you to become accepting and loving. To love some person, place, thing, idea, or event is to accept what you like and dislike about it. Communication is maximized in the love state. Whatever you are able to love builds love in you. People, places, things, ideas, and events are reflections of you.

COMMUNICATION ENHANCEMENT FORM

Perception of symmetry, proportion, and order leads us to truth.
The truth builds love and acceptance.

(+) Column 1: Positives or "goods." The omissions or commissions that you like and/or with which you are infatuated. ✦ The positive qualities, habits, character or personality traits you admire. ✦ Things that have attracted you to them. ✦ Things you would praise.	(+) Column 2: Episodes where and when you have been or done the same, somewhere in the seven areas of life. Think of any past or present person, place, thing, idea, or event.

*When positives outweigh negatives, you become attracted and infatuated. When negatives outweigh positives, you become repelled and resentful. When positives equal negatives (equal in degree, kind, magnitude, quantity, and quality), they **collapse** into each other, enlightening*

For free copies of this form, call (713) 334-0777 or write to:
Dr. Richard Bellamy, 2400 Augusta Drive, Suite 210, Houston, TX 77057

Person filling out form: _____

Person, place, thing, idea, or event attracted to or repelled from:

_____

The seven areas of life are:
physical, spiritual, mental, career, financial, family, and social.

(–) Column 3: Negatives or "bads." The omissions or commissions that you dislike and/or resent. ✦ The negative qualities, habits, character or personality traits you despise. ✦ Things that have repelled you from them. ✦ Things you would reprimand.	(–) Column 4: Episodes where and when you have been or done the same, somewhere in the seven areas of life. Think of any past or present person, place, thing, idea, or event.

you to become accepting and loving. To love some person, place, thing, idea, or event is to accept what you like and dislike about it. Communication is maximized in the love state. Whatever you are able to love builds love in you. People, places, things, ideas, and events are reflections of you.

COMMUNICATION ENHANCEMENT FORM

Perception of symmetry, proportion, and order leads us to truth.
The truth builds love and acceptance.

(+) Column 1: Positives or "goods." The omissions or commissions that you like and/or with which you are infatuated. ✦ The positive qualities, habits, character or personality traits you admire. ✦ Things that have attracted you to them. ✦ Things you would praise.	(+) Column 2: Episodes where and when you have been or done the same, somewhere in the seven areas of life. Think of any past or present person, place, thing, idea, or event.

*When positives outweigh negatives, you become attracted and infatuated. When negatives outweigh positives, you become repelled and resentful. When positives equal negatives (equal in degree, kind, magnitude, quantity, and quality), they **collapse** into each other, enlightening*

For free copies of this form, call (713) 334-0777 or write to:
Dr. Richard Bellamy, 2400 Augusta Drive, Suite 210, Houston, TX 77057

Person filling out form: _____

Person, place, thing, idea, or event attracted to or repelled from:

_____

The seven areas of life are:
physical, spiritual, mental, career, financial, family, and social.

(–) Column 3: Negatives or "bads." The omissions or commissions that you dislike and/or resent. ✦ The negative qualities, habits, character or personality traits you despise. ✦ Things that have repelled you from them. ✦ Things you would reprimand.	(–) Column 4: Episodes where and when you have been or done the same, somewhere in the seven areas of life. Think of any past or present person, place, thing, idea, or event.

you to become accepting and loving. To love some person, place, thing, idea, or event is to accept what you like and dislike about it. Communication is maximized in the love state. Whatever you are able to love builds love in you. People, places, things, ideas, and events are reflections of you.

COMMUNICATION ENHANCEMENT FORM

Perception of symmetry, proportion, and order leads us to truth.
The truth builds love and acceptance.

(+) Column 1: Positives or "goods." The omissions or commissions that you like and/or with which you are infatuated. ◆ The positive qualities, habits, character or personality traits you admire. ◆ Things that have attracted you to them. ◆ Things you would praise.	(+) Column 2: Episodes where and when you have been or done the same, somewhere in the seven areas of life. Think of any past or present person, place, thing, idea, or event.

*When positives outweigh negatives, you become attracted and infatuated. When negatives outweigh positives, you become repelled and resentful. When positives equal negatives (equal in degree, kind, magnitude, quantity, and quality), they **collapse** into each other, enlightening*

For free copies of this form, call (713) 334-0777 or write to:
Dr. Richard Bellamy, 2400 Augusta Drive, Suite 210, Houston, TX 77057

Person filling out form: _____

Person, place, thing, idea, or event attracted to or repelled from:

_____

The seven areas of life are:
physical, spiritual, mental, career, financial, family, and social.

(–) Column 3: Negatives or "bads." The omissions or commissions that you dislike and/or resent. ✦ The negative qualities, habits, character or personality traits you despise. ✦ Things that have repelled you from them. ✦ Things you would reprimand.	(–) Column 4: Episodes where and when you have been or done the same, somewhere in the seven areas of life. Think of any past or present person, place, thing, idea, or event.

you to become accepting and loving. To love some person, place, thing, idea, or event is to accept what you like and dislike about it. Communication is maximized in the love state. Whatever you are able to love builds love in you. People, places, things, ideas, and events are reflections of you.

About the Author

Dr. D. Richard Bellamy, philosopher and acknowledged expert in human potential technologies, is a dynamic and inspiring consultant, speaker, and seminar leader sought after around the world. He integrates an eclectic, wholistic, and unified approach in his highly successful work with clients on a diverse range of issues from personal to business.

Responses to this book are welcomed. If this book has had a significant impact on your life, please write to us and share your story.

Please contact Dr. Bellamy to schedule seminars and consultations, or to be on the mailing list for future events, by using any of the following:

write: Dr. Richard Bellamy
           2400 Augusta Drive, Suite 210
           Houston, TX 77057

call: toll-free (888) VIP-NOW1
           or (713) 334-0777

fax: (713) 334-6300

e-mail: Dr.Bellamy@Dr-D-Richard-Bellamy.com

web site: www.Dr-D-Richard-Bellamy.com

This book is also available on audio-cassette.

Persevere in your meaningful purpose with principled conceptualization, holding your vision continuously before you, with your calling within you, your feeling drawing you, your grand plan before you, your action expressed by you, with energy on your matter at hand, and gratitude for all that is, was, and will be.